Miracle at Candlestick!

The dramatic story of the San Francisco Giants'
amazing summer of '93—
of a season that almost wasn't, a team that
refused to quit, and a turnaround that
captured the imagination of an entire city.

TEXT BY NICK PETERS
PHOTOGRAPHY BY MARTHA JANE STANTON

LONGSTREET PRESS
Atlanta, Georgia

Published by LONGSTREET PRESS, INC.,
a subsidiary of Cox Newspapers,
a division of Cox Enterprises, Inc.
2140 Newmarket Parkway
Suite 118
Marietta, Georgia 30067

Printed in the United States of America

1st printing, 1993

ISBN: 1-56352-125-3

This book was printed by Arcata Graphics, Kingsport, Tennessee

Color separations by Holland Graphics, Mableton, Georgia

Editors: Grant Opperman, Erica Boeke, Jean Williams

The text was set in Stone Serif

Book and jacket design by Jill Dible

The front-cover photo collage for this book was assembled from three separate images by Giants Staff Photographer Martha Jane Stanton. In the center image, teammates lift Robby Thompson onto their shoulders after his ninth-inning home run beats the Florida Marlins, August 22nd at Candlestick Park.

Contents

A frequent sight at Candlestick Park in 1993.

The Year of Winning Dangerously

If the old saw, "It's not whether you win or lose, it's how you play the game" ever applied to a baseball season, it would define the Giants' uplifting pursuit of a division championship in 1993.

The rejuvenated Giants, infused with new blood and new hopes after nearly migrating to Florida just one year before, were like a blushing bride in a beautiful marriage between a baseball team and a grateful community.

It was a traditional wedding, actually. There was something old (veteran executive Bob Quinn), something new (superstar Barry Bonds), something borrowed (the capital to save the team) and something blue (ex-Dodger Dusty Baker).

From these pieces were forged an unforgettable season: 103 victories, the best record for a rookie manager in the history of the National League,

a remarkable 31-game improvement over 1992's record and a new franchise home attendance record of 2,606,354—up more than a million from '92.

Individual brilliance abounded, covering every facet of play. There was a franchise-record 48 saves by Rod Beck, 20-win seasons for both John Burkett and Bill Swift, an all-time Giants slugging percentage record of .677 by Bonds and a record-crunching errorless performance by center fielder Darren Lewis.

Off the field, the victories were just as impressive, as a group of investors

The Giants spent most of the 1993 season atop the National League West.

Fans celebrated another win from some of the best seats in the house—the newly-constructed left field bleachers.

Will Clark bear-hugged his new team-mate, Barry Bonds.

bursting with civic pride banded together to keep the Giants in Northern California.

"The San Francisco investors do not have what it takes, in terms of financial commitment, to get the deal done," a top baseball executive had said earlier, as the 11th hour approached. "This has been a charade from the start, with stalling tactics very much part of the strategy."

That doomsayer proved to be way off base. With the blessings of league owners who couldn't imagine San Francisco without a team, an investors' group headed by Walter Shorenstein and Peter Magowan got the job done.

But they weren't content with accepting congratulations and fielding a mediocre team in 1993. They realized how important it would be to make a dramatic improvement over last season's 72-90 debacle. So they made a dramatic move by signing baseball's best player, Barry Bonds, to the richest contract in baseball history—$43.75 million over six years.

The bold move, engineered by Magowan and Giants Executive Vice President Larry Baer before the Giants' sale was finalized, created such a media stir that even the fierce Joe Montana vs. Steve Young football rivalry was knocked off the Bay Area front pages and radio call-in shows.

That was just the tip of the iceberg, as far as improvements to the San Francisco Giants were concerned. There was also the hiring of a new

general manager to resolve. So, Bob Quinn, who had been named Major League Executive of the Year when his 1990 Cincinnati Reds posted a wire-to-wire division victory and swept the A's in the World Series, was hand-picked to succeed Al Rosen.

Shortly thereafter, Quinn named popular Hitting Coach Dusty Baker as manager. Bobby Bonds, a Giants hero from the past, joined his gifted son on

The Giants rang an authentic San Francisco cable car bell after each inning in which the home team scored.

The center field foghorn sounded for every Giants home run.

Score! Teammates congratulated Barry Bonds and Matt Williams as they crossed home plate.

BEST SAN FRANCISCO TEAMS

Year	Won/Lost	Pct.
1993	103-59	.636
1962	*103-62	.624
1965	95-67	.586
1966	93-68	.578
1989	*92-70	.568
1967	91-71	.562
1987	#90-72	.556
1971	#90-72	.556
1969	90-72	.556
1964	90-72	.556

*N.L. pennant

#N.L. West champion

THE NATIONAL LEAGUE'S BIGGEST 1993 IMPROVEMENTS

	1993	1992	Change
Giants	103-59	72-90	+31
Phillies	97-65	70-92	+27
Dodgers	81-81	63-99	+18
Expos	94-68	87-75	+7
Braves	104-58	98-64	+6
Cubs	84-78	78-84	+6

BEST ROOKIE MANAGERS

	Year	Won/Lost	Pct.
Houk, Yankees	1961	109-53	.673
Cochrane, Tigers	1934	101-53	.656
Baker, Giants	1993	103-59	.636
Howser, Yankees	1980	103-59	.636
Anderson, Reds	1970	102-60	.630

the club as Baker's coaching replacement. And Dick Pole, who had worked with Baker in the 1992 Arizona Fall League, was named pitching coach.

All the pieces were fitting perfectly in place, and the mood was festive during a December rally in Union Square when the old blended with the new and demonstrated their determination to turn the Giants from pretender to contender.

Baker was there. So were Bobby and Barry. Willie Mays and Orlando Cepeda were among those representing the glorious past. The new owners were gushing. Fans were excited. The celebration and enthusiasm signaled nothing less than a new beginning for the Giants and their ardent followers.

But the tell-tale signs of success went beyond mere pageantry. They became evident in Spring Training, where the new-look Giants assembled to hone their skills. Bonds was the focal point, but Quinn also brought in a host of new players like Dave Martinez, Todd Benzinger, Jeff Reed, Mark Carreon, Steve Scarsone, Paul Faries, and Luis Mercedes.

By the time Opening Day miraculously came again to Candlestick Park, fans had much more than just a Major League baseball team to cheer about. There were new left-field bleachers—some of the best seats in the park. Enthusiastic fans clamored for the chance at a seat in the sun and an up-close view of peerless outfielder Barry Bonds. The friendly voice of Sherry

Davis, baseball's first full-time female public address announcer, introduced the starting lineups. A green outfield wall replaced the cyclone fence of years past. And when Bonds homered in his very first home at-bat, Candlestick's center-field foghorn punctuated the occasion with a sonic blast—the first of many such celebrations to come in the 1993 season.

It was clear, this was going to be the

Sherry Davis, the new ballpark "voice" of the Giants, became baseball's first full-time female public address announcer.

LEFT—A young fan showed his enthusiasm for San Francisco's winningest team.
TOP—Fans enjoyed the sunshine at a Spring Training game in Scottsdale, Arizona.

BRAD MANGIN

Opening day at Candlestick Park, 1993.

Giants pitching aces Rod Beck (BELOW), John Burkett (LEFT) and Bill Swift (TOP) were major factors in the team's success.

place to be all summer long. With a schedule of 53 day games, second only to Wrigley Field, there was little talk now of the Candlestick weather, except to praise it. Gourmet food concessions were waiting to be discovered, too, from garlic-chicken sandwiches to barbecued ribs and dim sum. Even Candlestick employees seemed charged with a new spirit and enthusiasm and wore "We're Listening" buttons to solicit fans' suggestions.

And, oh, the baseball! The team that had struggled to a fifth-place finish in 1992 was now the talk of the Major Leagues. Six months and countless broken records later, the Giants found themselves at the center of one of

Giants president and managing general partner Peter Magowan shared a laugh with the team's newest acquisition, Barry Bonds.

New, improved Candlestick Park was the place to be in '93—with its new bleachers, out-of-town scoreboard, foghorn and outfield wall.

baseball's greatest finishes—one last pennant race for the ages, before divisional realignment in 1994. Heading into the season's final weekend, the Braves and Giants were deadlocked at a breathtaking 100 wins each.

It took three wins in a row at Dodger Stadium to remain tied on the final day of the season. Then, a 12-1 romp by Los Angeles shattered the Giants' championship dreams as dramatically as Trevor Wilson's 1991 shutout, Joe Morgan's 1982 homer, the 1962 playoff victory and Bobby Thomson's 1951 epic homer had all ruined L.A. titles in years past.

Still, the players headed home with heads high. "It hurts," a tearful Dave Burba said, unable to hide his emotion. "I'm thinking about how the guys on this club gave their heart and soul and came up short."

But it didn't take long for the sadness to ebb and for reality to set in. The Giants didn't have to apologize for a 103-59 record, the best in San Francisco history. "I'm a little ticked off and disappointed," Williams said. "When you win 103 games, you expect to win the whole thing. Unfortunately, the Braves are in the same division."

Beck quickly placed the season in perspective, less than one hour following the final out. He sat in the quiet clubhouse and reflected on a great season. "I'm not to the point where I feel we got cheated," Beck said. "You can't be ashamed when you win 103 games and you lose on the final day. We all realize what we accomplished."

Baker, who set an example all season by maintaining an even disposition through thick and thin, also was quick to place the bitter final defeat behind him. Shortly after the final out, he addressed the players and thanked them for a job well done.

"That's what life's about—how you handle hurt and disappointment," he said. "The guys gave me all they had. I told them not to be ashamed of anything and to walk proud. I was down

Manager Dusty Baker conferred with GM Bob Quinn.

when we got beat, but that lasted for about five minutes. Then I thought about the season and all we accomplished. I'll never forget it."

It was a memorable and magnificent season, brimming with fond memories for the team and its fans. As Baker suggested in May, "Baseball isn't a sprint; it's a marathon."

Well, the 1993 Giants made a gallant run. They set the early pace, fell back near the final hill, used a courageous finishing kick (14-2) to catch the leader and stumbled at the wire.

A great race, indeed.

Dusty Baker was introduced as the Giants' new manager at a December rally in San Francisco's Union Square.

The 1993 Giants took the field.

PART ONE

The Team

Dusty and his "dudes" discussed strategy.

CHAPTER ONE

Hitting Pretty

There was great anticipation in the final exhibition game of the spring, a victory over the cross-Bay A's, which showcased the Giants' offensive potential. A delighted Candlestick Park crowd watched Will Clark, Matt Williams and Barry Bonds, the new heart of the order, go deep. It didn't happen again all season, yet the point had already been made.

National League pitchers simply had to respect this Murderers Row and what it could mean to the complementary players surrounding them. The Giants' new-look offense would be a force to be reckoned with.

Was it ever! When the season concluded, the Giants led the league with a .276 batting average and a .427 slugging percentage. They ranked second with 808 runs and 168 home runs. Barry Bonds was primarily responsible for some of those imposing numbers,

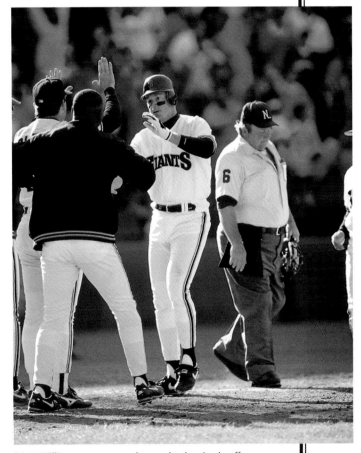

Matt Williams was among league leaders in six offensive categories: home runs, RBI, runs scored, slugging percentage, total bases and extra base hits.

The 1993 Giants boasted an unusually strong bench, including such capable subs as Mark Carreon (TOP), Dave Martinez (RIGHT), Todd Benzinger (PAGE 18) and Jeff Reed (PAGE 21.)

Dave Martinez

but his presence did much more. It raised the performance level of most of his teammates.

No fewer than five teammates followed his lead and enjoyed career years with a beautifully balanced offense that was reminiscent of the powerful teams of the 1960s. Bonds, himself, had never batted above .311 in a season and was a career .274 hitter until he exploded with a .336 aver-

age, second highest in San Francisco history behind Willie Mays' .347 in 1958.

And Bonds' batting increase of .062 over his lifetime average wasn't even the biggest on the club. Royce Clayton hiked his numbers 66 points to finish at .282. Robby Thompson soared .054 to .312. Williams batted .053 higher at .294 and hit a career-best 38 home runs.

Todd Benzinger

SAN FRANCISCO'S GREATEST ONE-TWO PUNCHES
(HR AND RBI)

Cepeda and Mays	1961	86-265=351
Mays and Cepeda	1962	84-255=339
Bonds and Williams	1993	84-233=317
Mitchell and Clark	1989	70-236=306
Mays and McCovey	1965	91-204=295
McCovey and Dietz	1970	61-233=294
McCovey and Bonds	1969	77-216=293

A GIANT IMPROVEMENT

The following shows how six Giants regulars
improved to career-best years in 1993:

	High*	Career	1993
Clayton	.224	.216	.282
Bonds	.311	.274	.336
Thompson	.271	.258	.312
Williams	.277	.241	.294
Manwaring	.244	.231	.275
Lewis	.248	.237	.253

*Former season high.

"There's no better lineup in the league," new Batting Coach Bobby Bonds declared early in the season. "I'm not surprised by what's happening. We have a lot of talent. A lot of our young players are just starting to come into their own. They're just beginning to scratch the surface. This offense will get a lot better."

The optimistic hitting coach watched the Giants score more than 10 runs four times in April, twice in May and June, and six times in a span of eight games in early July. Barry Bonds' all-around excellence was expected, but Williams' consistently high average and Thompson's lofty statistics were a mild surprise.

The offensive contributions of Clayton and Manwaring—and, for a while, of Darren Lewis—were startling. The Giants were like a well-oiled tank,

Kirt Manwaring established career highs in six batting categories, including average (.275), hits (119), home runs (5) and RBI (49).

Barry Bonds, Matt Williams and Will Clark showed heart in the middle of the Giants batting order.

steamrolling pitchers in their path. "With this offense, we don't fear any pitching staff," Bobby Bonds said. "Great pitching stops good hitting, but great hitting will hit good pitching."

Clark uncharacteristically struggled the entire first half, sinking to .218 in late May, but he still posed a threat in the number three hole and his teammates felt it was merely a matter of time. "Will's mechanics are too good for him to stay in a slump," Barry Bonds noted. "If we stay healthy, Will, Matt and I are capable of hitting 80-90 homers and driving in 300 runs."

Clark and Williams didn't remain

Jeff Reed

Robby Thompson received the crowd's applause after belting two home runs in a game for the second consecutive day.

healthy, yet Barry still was on target. In an off-year by Clark, the trio still accumulated 98 home runs and 306 RBI. "Fred McGriff bolstered the Braves and made them tougher in the middle of the order, but Atlanta doesn't compare with the Giants," Padres Batting Coach Merv Rettenmund said. "Bonds is an absolutely incredible player, and that's the difference."

Clayton contributed 70 RBI, matching Chris Speier for the most ever by a San Francisco shortstop. Thompson's 65 RBI were the most ever by a San

Royce Clayton hit a solid .282 and tied the San Francisco season RBI mark for shortstops, with 70.

Francisco second baseman, and he missed 34 games. Willie McGee quietly batted .301. Clark salvaged his season somewhat with consecutive four-hit games in must-win situations the final weekend. He batted .324 with 13 of his 14 home runs and 53 of his 73 RBI in his last 86 games, finishing at .283.

But the outstanding characteristic of this offense was its explosiveness. Ten or more runs were scored 17 times, at least six runs on 55 occasions. There were home runs in bunches, tape-measure homers and unprecedented power bursts. Bonds and Williams went back-to-back twice in the same game. Bonds had seven multiple-homer games; Williams had four.

Even Thompson got into the act. After never connecting twice in one game after seven years in the Majors, he did it on two consecutive June nights. Bonds drove in a career-high seven runs in one game; Williams and Clark had six-RBI splurges.

It was fun for everyone but the opposing pitchers, and it promises to get better because youth is on the Giants' side. If 1993 was a sneak preview, the rest of the 1990s figure to be a smash hit.

First-base Coach Bobby Bonds congratulated his son, Barry, after one of the younger Bonds' home runs.

In his last 12 games of the season, Will Clark batted .465 (20-for-43).

John Burkett and Bill Swift became the Giants' first 20-win tandem since Juan Marichal and Gaylord Perry in 1966.

The Men on the Mound

It was the biggest, most nagging question about the Giants: Could the team provide enough good pitching to support the newly improved offense? After all, the rotation wasn't set beyond the first couple of positions, and the team's history of injuries couldn't be far from anyone's mind as they looked at such '92 casualties as Bill Swift, Trevor Wilson and Bud Black.

But most of the Spring Training fretting was done by observers. Any doubts among the team were guised by expressions of confidence from Manager Dusty Baker, Coach Dick Pole, and the players.

"Our pitching is a lot better than people think," Baker cautioned one day in March. "With this offense, they're going to get more runs to work with, and that will make the job easier. Besides, we have a lot of quality and depth in the bullpen. If these starters give us six or seven innings, we'll be in good shape because I can turn it over to the relievers."

Righthander John Burkett looked at the rejuvenated offense during the exhibition games, liked what he saw and made a bold prediction that probably wasn't taken too seriously at the time. "I have the opportunity to pop

Mike Jackson was the Giants' most durable pitcher in 1993; his 81 appearances established a franchise and career high.

Buddy Black's season was shortened due to elbow problems. He did, however, post an 8-2 record in 1993 starts, including a five-game winning streak.

a great season," Burkett insisted. "I'm ready to get to a different level, and I think I can do it with this offense. I think I can win 20."

Burkett, who previously never won more than 14 games, exceeded even his own high expectations, posting a 22-7 season—the most victories by a Giant since Ron Bryant had 24 in 1973.

Baker proved prophetic, too. The Giants pitching staff posted a 3.61 earned run average, fifth in the National League, and the bullpen performed exactly as the rookie manager expected. With righthander Rod Beck obliterating the previous Giants saves record with 48 and Mike Jackson appearing in a league-leading 81 games as his set-up man, the bullpen was a strong suit most of the way.

There was legitimate concern over righthander Bill Swift's durability following an injury-scarred 1992 which resulted in a league-leading 2.08 ERA and merely 22 starts. But Swift, who had finished the previous season in the bullpen, felt compelled to start because he felt he was needed most in the rotation. It was an accurate and fortuitous assessment.

Swift stayed on the heels of Burkett all season—the two seemingly winning and losing in unison—and finished with a 21-8 record and a 2.82 ERA in a career-high and team-leading 232-and-two-thirds innings.

Will Clark and Barry Bonds also got in on the Spring Training predictions, mentioning that the Giants would go

Despite an injury-plagued season, Trevor Wilson posted a 4-2 record at Candlestick and a 3-3 record on the road.

Bryan Hickerson, showing his versatility as both a starter and set-up man, was a key ingredient of the Giants' pitching success.

Kevin Rogers had a 2-2 record with a 2.68 ERA in his first full year in the big leagues.

only as far as the health of the pitching staff would take them. They were wrong because success was plentiful despite injuries that limited left-handers Bud Black (8-2) and Trevor Wilson (7-5) to a total of 34 starts.

Baker and Pole performed a miracle with merely two healthy full-time starters, filling in the blanks deftly and finishing with a league-high 82

BEST SINGLE SEASON SAVE PERFORMANCES

PLAYER	YEAR	SV
Thigpen, W.Sox	1990	57
Myers, Cubs	1993	53
Eckersley, A's	1992	51
Smith, St. Louis-NY Yankees	1993	50
Beck, S.F	1993	48
Eckersley, A's	1990	48
Smith, Cards	1991	47

SAN FRANCISCO'S PREMIER PITCHING PAIRS

PLAYERS	YEAR	COMBINED RECORD
Marichal and Perry	1966	46-14
Burkett and Swift	1993	43-15
Sanford and O'Dell	1962	43-21
Marichal and Perry	1968	42-24
Marichal and Sanford	1963	41-21
Jones and Antonelli	1959	40-25
Marichal and Perry	1969	40-25

Rod Beck established a new Giants club record with his 48 saves for the season.

Opponents hit just .109 (17-for-86), lifetime against Jeff Brantley with the bases loaded; that career mark was the lowest in the Majors.

Greg Minton's franchise-record 30 saves were surpassed with two months to go. Beck had merely four blown saves while posting the second highest saves total (48) in National League history, exceeded only by Randy Myers' record 53 for the 1993 Chicago Cubs. Indeed, Beck was as close to perfection as a closer can get. He posted a 2.16 ERA and walked merely nine batters unintentionally in 79-and-one-third innings, striking out 86. He set the N.L. record with 24 consecutive successful save opportunities and finished the season with 16 in a row under extreme pressure.

"I'm not surprised by my success," said Beck, who landed on the All-Star team with Burkett. "I don't want to come off as arrogant, but I always expected this of myself. I'm fulfilling my dreams."

Catcher Kirt Manwaring agreed: "Rod is different because most stoppers have only one great pitch. He has three. He has one hell of a split, an outstanding breaking ball and a great fastball. He's got it all."

Beck also had a lot of help. Besides Jackson, who struck out 70 and walked 18 unintentionally in 77-and-one-third innings, the Giants also had solid results from Dave Burba (10-3) and rookie Kevin Rogers (2.68 ERA) out of the bullpen. They made it easier for Burkett and Swift to become the Giants' greatest one-two pitching punch since the days of Juan Marichal and Gaylord Perry.

Until the two aces did it in 1993,

victories by starters. The vaunted Atlanta Braves' rotation had 79 victories. "I've never worked with a greater group of guys," Pole said. "All of these guys have good work habits. There's a lot of talent here, and we have a good offense and defense supporting it."

Beck, a closer for less than a full season, and Jackson were the security blankets. Roles were defined. The eighth inning belonged to Jackson, and the ninth was Beck's. Used efficiently and effectively, they were the best bullpen tandem in the league.

Jim Deshaies, acquired from Minnesota on August 28, went 2-2 for the Giants in four starts.

the only other S.F. pitchers to each win 20 games in the same season were Hall of Famers Marichal and Perry in 1966. That also was the last time two National League teammates had 15 victories by August 1. Burkett and Swift attained that distinction and were a remarkable 35-9 after posting back-to-back victories on August 10-11. Comparisons were made to Marichal and Perry, and the present pair seemed embarrassed.

"That makes me laugh," Burkett said. "I'm not foolish enough to place

In 1993, Dave Burba posted seven wins in relief; he entered five of those games with San Francisco trailing.

Scott Sanderson has now notched a win over every Major League club except Colorado, which he had yet to face.

Veteran pitcher Dave Righetti worked in both the long-relief and set-up roles in 1993.

myself in that category. I'm just having a lot of fun and enjoying the ride."

Added Swift: "Marichal and Perry were big winners all the time, so it's a much bigger deal to us. I realize that I'm having a perfect season. The team is in first place and I'm having a career year."

The two starters simultaneously hit a wall and went winless over their next combined 11 starts as the Giants slipped out of first place. But they recovered down the stretch and fulfilled their 20-win dreams. Burkett won his last four starts, including eight innings of shutout pitching at Houston for his 20th victory, September 23. His 22 triumphs gave him 61 in four full seasons, a total exceeded in the N.L. only by Tom Glavine (72) and Greg Maddux (70) in the 1990s.

"Burkett pitches like you want guys to pitch," Pole said. "He throws strikes and uses both sides of the plate. A lot of guys have great pitches, but they can't get them over the plate. Burkett has a lot of good average pitches and he knows how to use them." Burkett went at least six innings in 28 of his 34 starts. He issued no walks in 13 games. He yielded two or fewer walks in 27 of his starts. He started 7-0 and added two five-game winning streaks.

Swift was even more impressive statistically. He had winning streaks of seven and six games, went at least six innings in 24 consecutive starts and in 29 out of 34 the entire season. He gave up two or fewer walks 28 times. And just when it seemed that fatigue would take its toll, Swift virtually was untouchable down the stretch—finishing the season with four consecutive victories in which he yielded two runs in 32 innings. He defeated the San Diego Padres 5-2 for win number 20, September 26.

"I never imagined I could win 20," said Swift, whose previous high had been 10. "In Spring Training, I was talking about winning 15. This is hard to believe. I caught a second wind, and now I have a better idea of what it takes."

Yet, with Black and Wilson out of action most of the second half, the Giants needed more than Burkett and Swift to remain competitive. Bryan Hickerson (7-5) and newcomers Scott Sanderson (4-2) and Jim Deshaies (2-2) provided a lift, and heralded rookie Salomon Torres (3-5) occasionally flashed the potential which made him the Giants' most promising minor league prospect.

"It would have been nice to have a healthy staff all season, but we gave it a go," Pole summed up. "Burkett and Swift did a great job. There were a lot of variables to having two 20-game winners.

"It starts with a solid bullpen. The starters knew that if they went six or seven innings, they'd have a good chance to win. It was the combination of quality pitchers performing to their potential. They threw strikes, didn't walk many and were supported by a solid offense."

Salomon Torres joined the big league club in August, in the heat of the pennant race. He posted a 3-5 record in eight starts.

Barry Bonds' play was admired by Giants fans in the left-field bleachers, who nicknamed their section "The Bonds Squad."

CHAPTER THREE

At the Top of Their Field

In recent years, the Giants have made excellent fielding a San Francisco trademark. By adding Barry Bonds and giving Darren Lewis full-time work, they truly dominated the National League on defense.

This happy fact was reflected both in the numerous spectacular plays afield and in the final statistics. With Bonds routinely turning doubles into singles with his strong play in left field, Lewis performing flawlessly in center, and former Gold Glove winner Willie McGee holding his own in right, the Giants at last had an outer defense to match the considerable infield strength. And the infield simply was beyond comparison—with past Gold Glove winners Matt Williams and Will Clark at the corners, Robby Thompson and Royce Clayton up the middle and Kirt Manwaring's strong arm behind the plate.

It all added up to all-time bests for the Giants, who set franchise records with just 101 errors and a league-leading .984 fielding percentage. "The Giants killed us this year [in eight out of 12 games], and the biggest difference was defense," said Philadelphia Phillies Coach Larry Bowa, a former record-setting shortstop. "They just didn't give you more than three outs,

Back-up catcher Jeff Reed threw out 42.9 percent of potential base-stealers in 1993 (12-of-28).

Steve Scarsone (TOP) and Mike Benjamin (BOTTOM) filled in admirably for ailing Giants infielders.

and they turned the double play."

The Giants, in fact, made 169 double plays to lead the league for a third consecutive year. That hadn't happened since the Pittsburgh Pirates did it nine years in a row, 1959-67. Thompson, who formed a great double-play combo with Jose Uribe for several seasons, continued his success with shortstop Royce Clayton, who played his first full Major League season in 1993.

"All the guys in the infield are important," said Bill Swift, a sinker-ball specialist. "But the double play is the key for a second baseman, and Robby is one of the best. He's one of the greatest I've ever seen."

JEFF CARLICK

Will Clark, the Giants regular first baseman for the past eight seasons, followed a foul ball into the photographers' pit.

Kirt Manwaring was the recipient of the 1993 Willie Mac Award, voted by his teammates as the Giants' most inspirational player.

Added John Burkett: "Robby is one of the most underrated players in the league, but not in this clubhouse. He hits, he turns the double play as well as anyone, and he's a leader." Thompson made only eight errors all season and was a steadying influence on Clayton, who made only 12 errors over his last 115 games following a shaky start.

Williams, like Bonds, a former Gold Glover whose hitting overshadows his fielding, once again displayed soft hands, quick reflexes and an accurate arm at third base. He

Royce Clayton (TOP) and Robby Thompson's (LEFT) skill at turning two helped the Giants lead the league in double plays for the third consecutive season.

Center fielder Darren Lewis established new Major League records for consecutive errorless games (316) and errorless chances by an outfielder (770).

made one-dozen errors and ranked second in the league with a .970 fielding percentage.

Manwaring, the strong, silent type, developed into one of the league's finest catchers in 1992. He continued his success from last season, leading the league with a .998 percentage. Manwaring made just two errors all season, deftly handled a vastly improved pitching staff and ranked second in the league by throwing out 42.3 percent of runners attempting to steal, 44 out of 104.

The outfield simply was the finest in San Francisco history. Bonds, Lewis and McGee all had speed, and McGee's full-time switch to right field made better use of his strong arm.

Matt Williams, a Rawlings Gold Glove Award winner in 1991, played spectacular defense.

Willie McGee (RIGHT) provided solid defense in right field; when he was disabled, Mark Carreon (TOP) was one of the subs who proved to be a fine replacement.

McGee led the team with nine outfield assists. But it was the graceful Lewis who commanded the most attention defensively. He went the entire season without an error in 131 games and 348 total chances, breaking two Major League records in the process. That set records for most consecutive errorless games and for most chances without an error by an outfielder, shattering standards previously held by Don Demeter and Curt Flood, respectively.

The modest Lewis played down his accomplishments, which include an ongoing streak of 316 games and 770 Major League chances without an error, but Bonds certainly took notice. "I played with (Gold Glove center fielder) Andy Van Slyke in Pittsburgh," Bonds said. "He's not quite in Andy's class yet, but he's getting there. It's just that Andy has done it much longer, and he has a rocket for an arm.

"But whereas Andy has to leave his feet and dive a lot to catch balls, D-Lew just runs them down. His greatest asset is his speed. Records or not, the guy is good with the glove."

Which is to say, he fit in perfectly with the rest of his teammates.

Willie McGee

Barry Bonds hit homer after homer after homer…and accepted congratulations time after time.

CHAPTER FOUR

The Homecoming King

When the Giants' new ownership group made a big splash by acquiring two-time National League MVP Barry Bonds as the cornerstone for its 1993 success, tradition was a part of it.

Linking the old with the new, the Giants also hired Bobby Bonds, Barry's father, as the batting coach. Bobby's Little League coach in Riverside was Johnnie Baker, new manager Dusty Baker's father.

There was an added connection because Willie Mays, perhaps the greatest Giant of them all, is Barry's godfather; the two developed a relationship in the Candlestick Park clubhouse 25 years ago.

What nobody realized was that Barry, who was drafted out of San Mateo's Serra High by the Giants in 1982, would make such a significant impact in his heralded homecoming.

Bonds enjoyed a season for the

Barry Bonds

Out in left field: Barry Bonds with ex-Giant Kevin Mitchell.

Bonds hit 46 home runs, his best-ever total.

ages, one he may never again approach, while justifying his $43.75-million contract and guiding the Giants to a San Francisco-record 103 regular-season victories.

"Can you imagine what Barry would have done if they had pitched to him?" Tony Gwynn of the San Diego Padres asked in September, noting Bonds' growing number of walks.

Bonds, batting fifth most of the season, walked 126 times. Only Len Dykstra of the Philadelphia Phillies, a leadoff hitter with 98 more at-bats, had more walks, 129.

Nobody came close to Bonds' 43 intentional walks — Larry Walker of the Montreal Expos was second with 20 — giving Barry the second highest number in baseball history, exceeded only by Willie McCovey's 45 in 1969.

But it wasn't the strolls to first base which set Bonds apart in 1993. It was his enormous all-around talent that included surges of power, bursts of speed and dazzling defense.

"I've never seen anyone like him," teammate Royce Clayton said early on. "He makes the game seem so simple. It's like he's playing Little League ball out there."

Bonds indeed made it look easy while leading the National League in virtually every important offensive category, including home runs (46) and runs batted in (123). In fact, his statistics would have earned him a Triple Crown in five out of the last seven seasons. No player has been able to lead the National League in average, RBI and home runs in the same season since Joe Medwick did it, in 1937.

He achieved a rare double, by lead-

A CAREER YEAR

Barry Bonds' remarkable consistency is apparent when glancing at his month-by-month accomplishments in 1993. He never batted below .280 or had a slugging percentage below .554 in any month.

	AB	R	H	Avg.	HR	RBI	Slug
April	72	23	31	.431	7	25	.889
May	98	24	36	.367	7	16	.684
June	93	12	26	.280	7	19	.559
July	91	23	28	.308	10	22	.692
Aug.	85	24	30	.353	8	19	.682
Sept.	92	19	27	.293	5	15	.554
Oct.	8	4	3	.375	2	7	1.200
1993	539	129	181	.336	46	123	.677

HOW BONDS RANKED IN 1993

Batting average	4th	.336*
Home runs	1st	46*
Runs batted in	1st	123*
Runs scored	2nd	129*
Hits	7th	181*
Total bases	1st	365*
Doubles	8th	38*
Bases on balls	2nd	126*
Intentional BB	1st	43*
On-base percentage	1st	.458*
Slugging percentage	1st	.677*
Extra-base hits	1st	88*
Games played	5th	159*
RBI per at-bat	1st	4.4*
HR per at-bat	1st	11.7*

*Career highs

ing in on-base percentage (.458) and slugging percentage (.677) in the same season, the latter figure setting an all-time Giants' record. The last time a player had led the National League in both categories was Stan Musial in 1948.

Godfather Mays held the old slugging standard of .667 with New York in 1954. The previous San Francisco record was .656 by Mays in 1965 and McCovey in 1969 during their MVP seasons.

Only Mays and Barry's father ever scored more runs in a San Francisco uniform. Only Mays and Kevin Mitchell hit more home runs in one season. Only the incomparable Mays had more total bases and extra-base hits.

"I've never had more fun in baseball," Bonds said. "I was fortunate to come up with a lot of guys on base and I felt strong most of the year. I was surrounded by good players and had a great time.

"There's no question this was my best year ever. Coming home was a part of it. I've never been more consistent. I didn't miss a lot of pitches. I was able to hit the mistakes."

Consistency was the key. Bonds, who entered the season with a .274 lifetime average, never batted below .280 in any month and was above .300 in five of the seven months.

"Barry gives you a different dimension because he can beat you with more than his bat," Gwynn observed. "I haven't seen anyone with Barry's

The second Bonds to wear number 25 for the Giants was introduced to Bay Area fans and media.

Bonds congratulated Robby Thompson after Thompson's game-winning homer vs. Florida in August.

Bonds refined his swing in Spring Training.

Barry coached his daughter, Shikari, before a Giants family softball game.

ability to wait on a pitch. With him, you take chances with Will Clark and Matt Williams, and they benefit."

Williams definitely flourished, having a career year along with Bonds. As the rejuvenated cleanup hitter, Williams batted .294 with 38 homers and 110 RBI. Bonds and Williams formed the best one-two punch in the league, combining for 317 home runs and RBI. Only Mays and Orlando Cepeda did better in S.F. history, totaling 351 in 1961 and 339 in 1962.

But Bonds' talent was never questioned. After all, he'd averaged 31 homers, 114 RBI and 45 stolen bases in 1990-92 while leading the Pittsburgh Pirates to three consecutive division titles.

The only questions raised were the

AN MVP SEASON

How Barry Bonds' 1993 season compared with the greatest years of other San Francisco sluggers. Three of the seasons earned MVP distinction and Bonds was a heavy favorite to make it four.

	Bonds	Mitchell	McCovey	Mays	Mays	Cepeda
	1993	1989#	1969#	1965#	1962	1961
Games	159	154	149	157	162	151
At-bats	539	543	491	558	621	585
Hits	181	158	157	177	189	182
Average	.336	.291	.320	.317	.304	.311
Doubles	38	34	26	21	36	28
Triples	4	6	2	3	5	4
Homers	46*	47*	45*	52*	49*	46*
Runs	129	100	101	118	130	105
RBI	123*	125*	126*	112	141	142*
Extra base hits	88*	87*	73	76	90*	78*
Total bases	365*	345*	322*	366*	382*	356*
Slugging percentage	.677*	.635*	.656*	.656*	.615	.609

#MVP *League leader

Bonds had 29 stolen bases in 1993, boosting his career total to 280.

result of a controversial personality caused by an outspoken demeanor and mood swings that sometimes left him misinterpreted and misunderstood.

Still, his extraordinary ability on a baseball field conquered all. When the Giants signed him following the 1992 season, Northern California was abuzz. It was a daring and stunning move that proved to be an off-season public relations coup.

"I'm shocked," Baker said upon hearing the news. "Getting Barry is unbelievable. He's an impact player. The organization made a statement to the world that they're serious about getting back into contention. The guy can flat-out play."

Willie McGee also was pleasantly surprised. He expressed feelings shared by many of the Giants who sorely needed a lift following the distractions and disappointment of 1992.

"Signing Barry was the last thing I expected," said McGee, a former MVP. "I'm surprised. None of us knew which way the organization would go. They showed everyone that they mean business.

"It pushes us up a notch. The whole objective is to place the best team on the field. It's a very positive move. They're definitely trying to get people in the stands. Bonds is one guy I'd pay to watch. He's definitely the most exciting player."

Baker and McGee were prophetic. Bonds lived up to all the expectations, and then some. The Giants became instant contenders when Bonds made

Willie Mays offered Spring Training advice to his godson, Barry Bonds.

Barry and his dad discussed life and hitting at first base.

Bonds led the Major Leagues in intentional walks, with 43.

Bonds was a 1982 graduate of Serra High School in San Mateo, California.

April a personal mission for acceptance.

He batted .431 with eight doubles, seven homers, 23 runs and 25 RBI the opening month. Bonds had an outrageous .889 slugging percentage and a .553 on-base percentage. The Giants took flight with him and were the early-season rage.

Most of the players around Bonds showed immediate improvement.

Williams batted .330 with eight homers in April. It didn't take long for Bonds to convince his new teammates that he was the real deal.

"Barry adds a new dimension," Williams said. "He creates opportunities for other guys and does the subtle things that go unnoticed. He seems to always know what the pitcher has on his mind."

Will Clark shared a laugh in the dugout with new teammate Bonds.

Baker was elated. The new owners gave him a better chance to win by adding Bonds, so making out the lineup card was truly a pleasure instead of a chore.

"Because of Barry, we're a better club now than we were a couple of years ago," said Baker, the batting coach of the 1989 pennant-winners. "Barry gives us Mitchell's power, plus speed and a higher average.

"We're capable of doing a lot more now because of what he brings to the team. Matt is a much better hitter now and Barry is the best all-around player in the league."

Bonds continued his early-season surge and was the fans' top vote-getter for the All-Star team. At the break, Barry was batting .348 and leading the league with 24 homers and 71 RBI. Not coincidentally, the Giants were 59-30 with a nine-game lead.

"We did what we wanted in the first half," Bonds said. "Now we have to forget about it and go from there."

An intense Barry Bonds looked ahead to the '93 season.

Barry Bonds settled into his home run trot.

Bonds did his part. Despite 16 fewer games after the All-Star break, he came through with 22 more home runs and 52 more RBI despite a two-week power slump in early September and a steady number of walks.

When the division race heated up once again down the stretch, Bonds delivered six homers and 18 RBI in the final 11 games, nine of them victories. The outburst included his seventh two-homer game of the season and a career-high seven RBI at Dodger Stadium, October 1.

Bonds' amazing season had everything but a championship ring. There were career highs in virtually every category, Gold Glove defensive plays on a frequent basis, 103 victories and adoring fans and appreciative teammates. A dream season, indeed.

Top Giants sluggers discussed strategy.

Giants players looked ahead to a challenging season.

PART TWO

The Season

Bill Swift, a 21-game winner, far exceeded his Spring Training prediction of 15 wins.

CHAPTER FIVE

Enchanted April

BY THE NUMBERS
April Accolades
Record: 15-9, first-place tie.

Batting leaders:
Bonds, .431, 7 HRs, 23 runs, 25 RBI.
Williams, .330, 8 HRs, 22 runs, 18 RBI.

Pitching leaders:
Burkett, 5-0, 2.62 ERA, 34-and-one-third IP, 26 hits.
Beck, 2-1, 2.35 ERA, 7 SV, 20 SO, 2 BB.

Outstanding performances:
Bonds, National League Player of the month.
Thompson, 4 hits, 4 RBI at N.Y., 4/22.
Williams, 4 hits, 2 HR vs. Braves, 4/18.
Bonds, 3 hits, 5 RBI vs. Braves, 4/15.
Bonds, 4 hits, 3 2B vs. Braves, 4/18.
Bonds, 3 hits, 2 HRs, 4 RBI vs. Mets, 4/29.

According to the wizards of baseball, it's how you finish the season that counts, not how you start it. In the case of the 1993 Giants, there was an exception to the rule.

If any team ever required a quick getaway, it was the Giants. With new ownership and a new superstar, they needed instant credibility with their baseball fans, who were still recovering from the off-season specter of the team's near-move to St. Petersburg. The Giants had to prove immediately that they were still worthy of undying support.

They got even more than they had hoped for with a 15-9 April, which catapulted the team into a first-place tie with the Houston Astros and made a terrific first impression. Opening Night in St. Louis was a harbinger of what was to come. A crowd of 50,269 gathered at Busch Stadium, and the new-look Giants spoiled the party in most appropriate fashion. Newcomer Dave Martinez scored the first run and Barry Bonds hit a sacrifice fly to drive in the second in a 2-1 victory behind the pitching of John Burkett and Rod Beck. The Giants dropped the series, but won two out of three in Pittsburgh to come home with a 3-3 record. A 14-hit, 12-5 romp against the Pirates set the stage for one of the club's most memorable homecomings.

Manager Dusty Baker sized up his 1993 squad.

Opening Day at refurbished Candlestick Park, April 12, was a rousing success on two fronts. An overflow crowd of 56,689 was the largest ever to attend a home opener in San Francisco. The anxious fans weren't disappointed; besides enjoying the improved concessions, the new left-field bleachers and baseball's first female P.A. announcer, they were treated to a Bonds home run on his first home at-bat. In the end, the Giants posted a 4-3 victory over the Florida Marlins on 10th-inning singles by Mike Benjamin and Darren Lewis.

The Giants won the opening series and braced for the invasion of the defending champion Atlanta Braves for a four-game series that was viewed as an early test of the club's character. On Thursday night, converted reliever Jeff Brantley yielded just one run in seven-and-two-thirds innings and

Barry Bonds homered in his first Candlestick Park at-bat as a San Francisco Giant.

Bonds blasted a three-run homer in the first inning off Greg Maddux, propelling the Giants to an easy 6-1 victory. Bonds, who finished with five RBI, doubled and scored on Kirt Manwaring's single the next night in support of John Burkett's 1-0 victory.

The Braves averted a sweep when Steve Avery's Saturday shutout performance, along with Terry Pendleton's ninth-inning homer, produced a 2-0 victory. In the Sunday finale, the Giants demonstrated their comeback abilities by overcoming 5-0 and 11-6 deficits. They also survived a brief shower of giveaway "fotoballs" which fans had thrown onto the field to protest a Braves scoring surge. The game came down once again to extra innings, with Matt Williams blasting a Steve Bedrosian pitch out of the park in the 11th to cap a 13-12 victory. No doubt about it, these Giants were for real.

A 4-4 trip to New York, Montreal and Philadelphia was another early test, with the Giants giving a hint of their character during the two-game series with the Phillies. In the opener at Veterans Stadium, April 26, the Giants parlayed 10 walks and seven hits into an 8-0 lead by the sixth inning. Brantley seemed in complete control with a three-hitter. Then it turned ugly.

The Phillies chipped away with three runs in the bottom of the sixth, capitalized on three walks for four more runs in the seventh and tied it in

April's National League Player of the Month, Barry Bonds.

Kirt Manwaring had a career-high 10-game hitting streak from April 10-21.

GAME OF THE MONTH

The victory on the heels of the Phillies' comeback was inspirational, but the win that defined the Giants' April occurred against the mighty Braves, April 18, before 37,264 at Candlestick Park.

Atlanta needed a victory for a split of the opening four-game series and unbeaten Tom Glavine was on the mound. A laugher was in the works when the Braves jumped on Dave Burba for five runs in the top of the first.

But there was an immediate hint that this was to be a special season for the Giants. Kirt Manwaring's two-run double helped them score three runs in the second. Bonds' run-scoring double chased Glavine in a three-run third for a 6-5 Giants' lead.

The Braves rallied for six runs in the fourth off Bryan Hickerson and rookie Kevin Rogers. Greg Olson's three-run homer crowned the rally, giving Atlanta an 11-6 lead. Still, the Giants weren't done. Matt Williams homered off Greg McMichael in the fifth. Darren Lewis' double and Bonds' single made it 11-8 off Pete Smith in the seventh.

Sid Bream doubled for his fourth RBI as Atlanta went ahead 12-8 in the eighth, but the Giants rallied once again off Mike Stanton and Jay Howell in the bottom of the ninth. Williams' run-scoring single and Bonds' RBI-double got things going one more time, and sacrifice flies by Robby Thompson and pinch-hitter Todd Benzinger created a 12-12 tie.

The comeback was too sweet to let this one get away. It didn't. Williams' leadoff homer off ex-Giant Steve Bedrosian in the bottom of the 11th produced a memorable 13-12 victory, among the highlights of a memorable season.

"That's probably one of the strangest games I've ever been involved with," a weary Glavine said. "I'm ready to get out of here."

Matt Williams hit a game-winning homer April 18 against the Braves.

Giants players waited their turns in fielding drills.

the eighth. Manager Dusty Baker's worst fears were realized when Gino Minutelli's wild pitch with two outs in the bottom of the 10th gave the delirious Phillies an improbable 9-8 victory.

The Giants were stunned. Burkett, who was to pitch the trip finale, was back at the hotel, fast asleep. He went to bed thinking the team had won, and it wasn't until the next morning, that he heard the bad news. But Burkett and his teammates didn't dwell on the defeat. He blanked the Phillies for five innings, Will Clark had a two-run double, Williams homered and Bonds slashed a two-run triple in a 6-3 victory over Terry Mulholland.

"What happened the other night

Closer Rod Beck was 2-1 with seven saves in April.

Jeff Brantley warmed up, as Pitching Coach Dick Pole looked on.

Robby Thompson had the finest year by a second baseman in S.F. Giants history.

might have been the best thing," Baker said of the Phillies' comeback. "It was a wake-up call for all of us. I told the guys the next day to give me nine innings, not six."

Revived, the Giants returned home to win their last three games of the month for a successful April, one which showcased the immense talent of Bonds and made fans and management alike realize that they had gotten a bargain in baseball's highest-paid player.

Bonds earned National League Player of the Month distinction a second straight time following a brilliant September with the 1992 Pirates. He batted .431 with 25 RBI and an .889 slugging percentage in his first month with the Giants.

His success was contagious. Williams rebounded from a disap-

Barry Bonds met the press.

pointing 1992 to bat .330 with eight home runs in April. Burkett, who had predicted 20 wins in Spring Training, was already one-fourth of the way there at 5-0.

Beck firmly established himself as a quality reliever in under one year on the job. He was 2-1 with seven saves in April, striking out 20 batters and walking merely two in 15-and-a-third innings.

"You have to have the mentality that they can't touch you," Beck said of his early surge. "If you don't have that attitude, you can't be as successful as you'd like."

The Giants' newest star.

A rejuvenated Will Clark got seven hits in the Giants' three-game May series in Atlanta.

CHRIS HAMILTON

CHAPTER SIX

Life at the Top

BY THE NUMBERS
The Merry Month of May
Record: 18-9,
four-and-a-half game lead.

Batting leaders:
McGee, .375, 36 hits, 7 2B.
Bonds, .367, 7 HR, 24 runs, 16 RBI.
Thompson, .320, 8 2B, 22 runs.
Williams, .284, 7 HR, 16 runs, 25 RBI.

Pitching leaders:
Swift, 4-1, 3.03 ERA

Outstanding performances:
Thompson, 20-game hitting streak.
Williams, 4 hits vs. Dodgers, 5/7.
Williams, 15-game hitting streak.
Bonds, 4-for-4, 3 runs vs. Phillies, 5/5.
Black, 3-hitter, 8 IP at Denver, 5/12.
Swift, 3-hitter, 8 IP vs. Reds, 5/21.

Following an opening month in which they raised hopes, the Giants continued to look more like contenders than pretenders with a solid May that bolstered their confidence, saw them build a four-and-a-half game lead in the standings and helped them earn respect around the league.

"The Giants aren't a surprise to me," Braves Manager Bobby Cox said after the Giants won two out of three in Atlanta at the end of May. "They've always been a good defensive club, and then you add Barry Bonds, who gives you a glove and a bat.

"I always felt Matt Williams gives you so much defense, you'd be happy to get .240-.250 out of him with 20 homers and 80 RBI. And I hope when Will Clark wakes up, the others go to sleep."

Cox's worst fears were realized. Clark woke up with seven hits in the three-game Atlanta series, and other Giants continued to produce throughout an 18-9 May that gave San Francisco the Western Division lead.

Still, there was an air of caution about the Giants' early-season success. Just one year earlier, they had a solid 27-21 record on June 1 and were in a first-place tie. Then the 1992 team unraveled, going 2-6, 4-13 and 6-17 to fall to nine-and-a-half games back. By contrast, the

In May, Willie McGee thrived in the number six hitting spot.

1993 Giants used the month of May to gain momentum by going 10-1 in the middle of the month, including a season-high seven-game winning streak.

And this time, the strong start simply felt different. The Giants seemed in much better shape, having built a 33-18 record after the first two months of 1993. They did it with improvement in all facets of the game—boosting their batting average, improving their pitching and proving their defense to be one of the league's best.

Offensively, the batting order clicked on all cylinders with the help of Clark's rejuvenation. "It's nice to get Will going," said Bonds, who himself enjoyed a .367 May. "Your number three hitter is always important. He's the guy who sets the table."

Several Giants feasted in May. The

PHIL DAVIS

Kirt Manwaring displayed great defense as he prevented an Atlanta run.

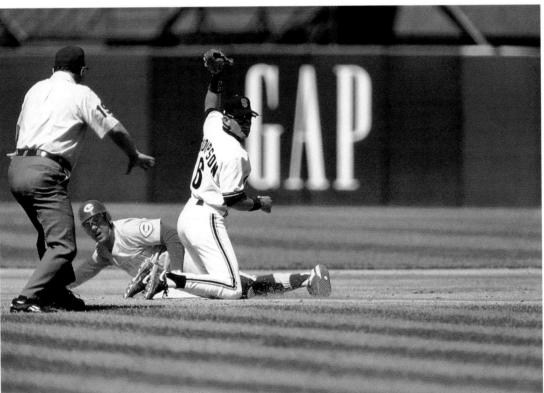

Royce Clayton (TOP) replaced Jose Uribe as Robby Thompson's (BOTTOM) double-play partner.

GAME OF THE MONTH

As had been the case at Candlestick Park in late April, the Giants needed a victory at Fulton County Stadium, May 30, to win another showdown with the Braves (this time a three-game series) and to continue their early season dominance of the defending N.L. champs. Once again, Tom Glavine stood in their way, along with 48,886 tomahawk-chopping partisans.

Rod Beck finished things off with a scoreless ninth.

PHIL DAVIS

Burkett was handed his first loss of the season following seven victories in the series opener, but rookie Greg Brummett evened the series score with a 6-3 victory on national TV. That left it up to Glavine and Jeff Brantley in the rubber match.

Just like in the previous series in San Francisco, the Braves staked Glavine to a lead. They scored single runs in the second, third and fourth innings for a 3-0 lead off Brantley, before a one-out homer by Robby Thompson ruined Glavine's shutout bid in the fifth.

Thompson again was the catalyst in the seventh. He led off and was safe at first on third baseman Terry Pendleton's error. Will Clark singled and Matt Williams flied to right. Then, Barry Bonds burned Atlanta by hitting an 0-1 pitch over the fence in right for a 4-3 lead that held up behind the shutout relief of Kevin Rogers, Mike Jackson and Rod Beck. The bullpen finished the month with one run relinquished in 27-and-two-thirds innings.

"He put it in the right spot," Bonds said of the high-and-inside Glavine fastball that turned the game. "Anytime you do it against Glavine, you've got to be happy. He's their big guy, and he made just one mistake."

PHIL DAVIS

Barry Bonds burned Atlanta with a blast to right field, giving San Francisco a 4-3 lead.

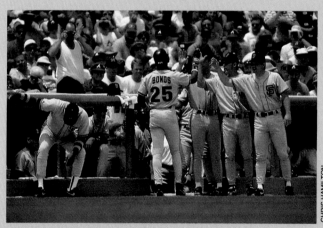

CHRIS HAMILTON

Bonds and his teammates celebrated his homer.

team batted .294 to climb from fifth to first in the National League. They averaged 5.3 runs per game for the month.

Willie McGee thrived in the number six spot, protecting Bonds and batting .375. Robby Thompson batted .320 and finished the month with a 20-game hitting streak.

The expansion Colorado Rockies contributed mightily to the offensive resurgence. While winning three out of four at Mile High Stadium, May 10-13, the Giants had runners on base in 35 of 36 innings, scored 30 runs and batted .372—lifting the team batting average from .266 to .279.

"It's a good hitter's park," observed Matt Williams, who extended his hitting streak to 15 games. But it wasn't a bad pitcher's park, either, for the Giants. Starters Bill Swift, Bud Black and John Burkett each posted victories, yielding merely seven runs in 22-and-a-third innings.

The pitching staff had ranked seventh with a collective 3.70 earned run average in April. The ERA improved to 3.31 in May, placing the Giants among the team leaders. Yet, most of the improvement was in the bullpen. The relievers posted a 1.77 earned run average in May and had five saves in five opportunities. Big leads at the end of games prevented more saves.

A defense that had ranked eighth at the end of April improved statistically as shortstop Royce Clayton

Dave Burba began his eight-game winning streak—the longest by a Giants pitcher since 1989—on May 17.

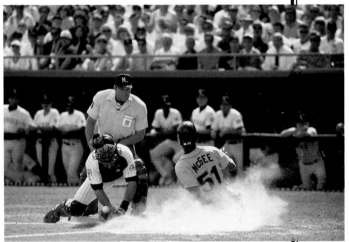

The Giants' offense surged in Colorado; here, Willie McGee slid safely into home.

drastically reduced his errors. Suddenly, there were no holes. The comparisons with last year was revealing.

The 1992 Giants ranked 11th among 12 teams in batting average (.244) and runs per game (3.5). As June began, the Giants were first with a .280 average and second with 5.1 runs.

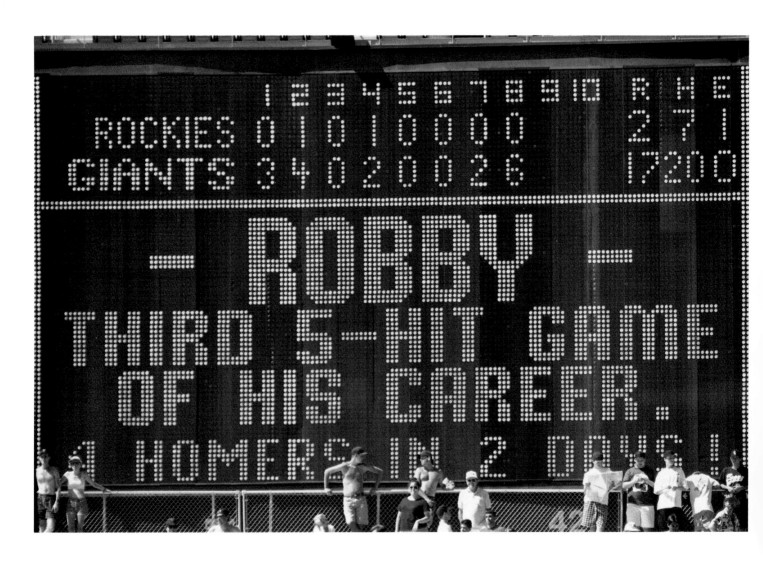

CHAPTER SEVEN

A Month to Remember

I t was a month for doubters to behold. Just wait 'til June, they had warned—perhaps thinking of the Giants' 7-19 fall from grace the previous year. These Giants, however, emphatically placed to rest all notions of a swoon by going 19-9 and adding three games to their division lead over the Atlanta Braves. By July 1, they were ahead by seven-and-a-half games and still accelerating toward the

---

BY THE NUMBERS
A June Boon
Record: 19-9, seven game lead.

Batting leaders:
Thompson, .398, 39 hits, 22 runs, 15 RBI.
Clark, .289, 16 runs, 18 RBI.
Bonds, .280, 7 HR, 19 RBI.
Williams, .250, 6 HR, 21 RBI.

Pitching leaders:
Burkett, 5-1, 2.70 ERA, 28 SO, 3 BB.
Black, 4-0, 1.36 ERA.
Swift, 4-2, 2.66 ERA.
Wilson, 3-1, 3.38 ERA.
Beck, 0.84 ERA, 10 SV, 15 SO, 2 BB.

Outstanding performances:
20 team hits in 17-2 rout of Rockies, 6/24.
McGee, 4-for-4 vs. Padres, 6/21.
Thompson, 5-for-5, 3 RBI vs. Cubs, 6/12.
Thompson, four HRs in 2 days, 6/23-24.
Williams, 6 RBI, 2B, HR at Houston, 6/19.
Swift, 1-hitter, 8 IP, at Cincy, 6/17.
Swift, 2-hitter, 8 IP, vs. Rockies, 6/27.

No June Swoon

Though the "June Swoon" is more myth than fact, the 1993 Giants erased all doubts that they would fade early by posting a 19-9 record—for the second most successful June in San Francisco history. Here are the top five since 1958:

1990	19-8	.704
1993	19-9	.679
1989	18-10	.643
1964	19-11	.633
1966	18-12	.600

All-Star break.

June swoon indeed; June Boon would be more like it. Unlike May, when a .294 team batting average spurred an 18-9 month, the Giants turned to stout pitching in the second best June in San Francisco history.

"Starting pitching obviously was the key," Manager Dusty Baker said. "But the defense also rose to the level we expected all along."

Fielding improved noticeably

Robby Thompson smacked four home runs in two days in June; he also batted .357 with a team-high 35 hits.

during the month—shortstop Royce Clayton made just one error, for instance—but it was the starting pitching which commanded most attention.

The rotation core of John Burkett (5-1), Bud Black (4-0), Bill Swift (4-2) and Trevor Wilson (3-1) was an impressive combined 16-4 with a 2.54 earned run average.

Bullpen stopper Rod Beck was needed for only 10-and-two-thirds innings the entire month, yet he made the most of his opportunities with a 0.84 ERA and 10 saves. Collectively, the pitching staff posted a tidy 2.85 ERA in June.

"The biggest difference in the Giants this year is the pitching," former teammate Brett Butler of the Los Angeles Dodgers said of the transformation. "The offense is no better than it was when we went to the World Series in 1989. Barry Bonds has been great for them, but it's tough to have a better year than Mitch [Kevin Mitchell] had in 1989. There's just more pitching depth and more balance on this year's team."

Long-time Giant-killer Eric Davis, who faced the 1987 and 1989 champion Giants as a member of the Cincinnati Reds, also noticed a big difference when facing the 1993 version. "These Giants have much better pitching," Davis said. "The 1987 and 1989 clubs were built on offense. Now, they have the pitching, and that's what championships are built on. It seems like every time

Trevor Wilson also helped out offensively, with a June 5 homer against the Pirates.

Pitching Coach Dick Pole said he wasn't surprised at the success of his hard-working pitching staff.

BRAD MANGIN

Black (LEFT), Swift (RIGHT), Wilson and Burkett had a combined 16-4 record in June.

the Giants score three or four runs, they win."

Among the 28 games in June, Giants' pitchers contained the opposition to two runs or fewer in 15 of them. Starters went at least seven innings 16 times, giving the bullpen a mid-season rest.

"I've never been around such a group of quality guys," first-year Pitching Coach Dick Pole said. "These pitchers give themselves the best chance to succeed because they work so hard as a group. I can't say I'm surprised by the results. The starters, as a whole, are not walking a lot of people.

Swift and Burkett don't throw a lot of pitches, so they're eating up innings. Black had a great month, too. He's mixing his pitches well to make his fastball look better. The starters have done so well, it's been difficult to get the bullpen guys innings."

A bigger concern for Baker was the dwindling middle-of-the-order punch with injured Matt Williams out of the lineup. Bonds was getting fewer pitches to hit, but Will Clark showed positive signs in June by batting .289 with 18 RBI. Bonds slipped to .280 in June, yet had 19 RBI and a team-leading seven home runs. Williams, despite

Trevor Wilson

BRAD MANGIN

John Burkett

missing several games, added six homers and 21 RBI.

Robby Thompson picked up the slack with an explosive month—batting .357 in June with a team-high 35 hits.

He had five home runs—including an awesome four in two days against the Padres and the Rockies—and 15 RBI.

In those two games, June 23-24, Thompson erupted for seven hits in 10 at-bats, four homers, six runs and five RBI. The power surge obscured a Bonds grand-slam in the 20-hit, 17-2 pounding of the Rockies.

"I'm obviously feeling pretty good at the plate," Thompson said of his Ruthian performance. "It all started when we visited Denver in May. I was struggling, but I had a good series (7-for-16) and went on a 21-game hitting streak. I got into a groove."

All an astonished Baker could add was, "Robby is locked in right now. You can see it. The ball looks big to him and his confidence level is at an all-time high."

All over the Bay Area, fans could be heard saying the same of the San Francisco Giants.

GAME OF THE MONTH

The June highlight was a 5-1 trip to Cincinnati and Houston, usually tough places for the Giants to play. It seemed like this trip would be no exception when the Giants began the trip with a crushing 10-5 loss to the Reds, June 15 at Riverfront Stadium. The pounding was punctuated by a 17-hit Cincinnati attack.

One day later, Reds ace Jose Rijo carried a 3-2 lead into the seventh inning and retired the first two batters he faced. Then Dave Martinez, who had homered in the second inning, did it again for a 3-3 tie. Pinch-hitter Randy Milligan's single gave the Reds a 4-3 lead in the bottom of the seventh off Trevor Wilson, setting the stage for one of the most dramatic ninth innings of the season.

Reds relief ace Rob Dibble was summoned to protect the lead. He retired Will Clark and Matt Williams. The Giants seemed dead. One pitch away from a save, Dibble gave Barry Bonds something he could hit. It was power versus power, and Bonds won by powering the ball over the fence in center field for a game-tying homer. "Barry is awesome to watch," teammate Darren Lewis said on a night when Bonds was at a loss for words. "I'm glad just to be a part of it."

The Giants weren't finished with their two-out heroics, though. After Benny Ayala retired the first two batters in the 10th, Lewis beat out an infield hit and went to third on Robby Thompson's single to center.

Greg Cadaret replaced Ayala and was greeted by Clark's tie-breaking single to left. Williams added a run-scoring single to left, and the Giants needed it because of a worrisome bottom of the 10th.

Rod Beck yielded a pair of singles and a sacrifice fly to Roberto Kelly. With the tying run on third base and two outs, Beck then struck out Chris Sabo for his 20th save and one of the Giants' most inspiring victories of the season.

BRUCE CRIPPEN

Barry Bonds hit a game-tying blast against Cincinnati.

Dave Martinez helped his team out with two homers.

Rod Beck (TOP AND ABOVE) is congratulated by relieved catcher Kirt Manwaring after a heart-pounding 10th inning.

In July, both Barry Bonds (LEFT) and Darren Lewis batted over .300.

CHAPTER EIGHT

The Balancing Act

BY THE NUMBERS
A Giant July
Record: 19-9,
seven-and-a-half game lead.

Batting leaders:
Manwaring, .377, 14 RBI.
Clayton, .333, 21 RBI.
Bonds, .308, 10 HR, 23 runs, 22 RBI.
Lewis, .300, 21 runs, 14 RBI.
Clark, .299, 19 runs, 13 RBI.

Pitching leaders:
Swift, 5-1, 2.08 ERA, 32 SO.
Burba, 3-0, 3.20 ERA.
Burkett, 3-1, 3.44 ERA.
Beck, 7 saves, 1.46 ERA, 13 SO, 1 BB.

Outstanding performances:
Swift, N.L. Pitcher of the Month.
Team batted .296, averaged 5.4 runs.
McGee, 4 hits, 3 RBI at Montreal, 7/5.
Clark, 4 hits, 3 runs at Montreal, 7/6.
Bonds, 6 RBI, 2 HRs at Philly, 7/8.
Bonds, two doubles in All-Star Game.
Scarsone, 10 hits, 7 RBI at Philly, 7/8-11.
Manwaring, four-for-four, HR, 3 RBI at
  Denver, 7/30.
Team scores 74 runs in 8 games, 7/4-11.
23 hits at Philly, 7/9; 68 in 4 games.
Burkett, 3-hitter, 8 IP vs. Dodgers, 7/27.

JULY'S PERSONAL BESTS

Despite injuries to several key players, the
Giants posted their best July record ever in
San Francisco. How they rated:

1993 18-8, .692
1972 16-8, .667
1990 17-10, .630
1991 15-9, .625
1969 18-11, .621

In a game where sustained excellence is a rarity, the 1993 Giants set new standards for consistency and success during the best July in their 36-year San Francisco history.

The remarkable month saw San Francisco chalk up 18 wins and just eight losses, despite injuries that knocked Matt Williams, Robby Thompson, Willie McGee, Bud Black, Trevor Wilson and Mike Jackson out of action. "What we did in July is a little surprising under the circumstances," Manager Dusty Baker said. "There's no question it was a key month. Looking at the schedule in Spring Training, we felt July would be the toughest month because we had our longest trip of the season."

What Baker couldn't possibly have anticipated were injuries that kept three regulars, two starting pitchers and a bullpen workhorse out of com-

San Francisco was represented at the 1993 All-Star Game by, L-R, Rod Beck, Robby Thompson, Barry Bonds and John Burkett.

Steve Scarsone, who came to the Giants in a late-Spring Training trade, excelled as an infield replacement.

mission for parts of the month. Still, the club continued its winning ways by getting big contributions from unexpected sources. Steve Scarsone, for instance, filled in with a .355 average and 11 RBI for the month. Kirt Manwaring, providing an offensive bonus much of the season, batted .377 with 14 RBI in July. Royce Clayton had a .333 average and 21 RBI for the month. Darren Lewis batted .300 with 21 runs.

Those complementary players augmented the heart of the order and nearly overshadowed the achievements of Barry Bonds, who batted .308 with 10 homers, 23 runs and 22

RBI for the month. It all added up to a solid .296 batting average and 151 runs (5.8 per game) in July, compensating for a slight pitching slump that produced a 3.80 team earned run average for the month.

"We're such a good offensive team, we would have to have a great month of pitching thrown against us to slow us down," Batting Coach Bobby Bonds said. "We have too many good hitters throughout the batting order to go through long dry spells. Plus we have the pitching to keep us in games. I really don't think we'll have a major slump."

The Giants were sternly tested in July when they faced the Philadelphia Phillies, the N.L. East leaders, a total of eight times. The Giants passed with flying colors, winning six of those games. Three of the victories came without the services of Williams and Thompson for a four-game series with the East-leading Phillies at Veterans Stadium prior to the All-Star break. The Giants outscored the Phillies 41-20 in the series, batting .398. They entered the All-Star break with a 59-30 record and a nine-game lead over the Braves.

"We're in the wrong division," Braves pitcher Glavine lamented at the All-Star Game, where his teammates included Bonds, Thompson, John Burkett and Rod Beck. Bonds received 3,074,603 fans' votes, the most for an individual player since 1980. The Giants had the best record at the break in San Francisco history, led the Majors with a .288 batting average and ranked second in pitch-

Once again a reliever, Jeff Brantley maintained a 1.84 ERA in July.

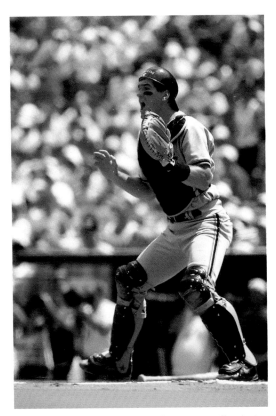
Kirt Manwaring had an outstanding season offensively, as well as behind the plate.

Bryan Hickerson excelled as a starter in July.

ing with a 3.42 earned run average.

When regulars were injured, Scarsone played a key role as an infield replacement, but the pitching staff also had some unsung heroes in an emergency. Swing man Bryan Hickerson went 3-1 as a starter. Dave Burba was 3-0 in July. They complemented the one-two punch of Bill Swift and Burkett, who were a combined 8-2. Swift earned N.L. Pitcher of the Month honors with a 5-1 record and a 2.08 ERA.

Despite Jackson's injury, the bullpen didn't falter. Jeff Brantley returned to relief and had a 1.84 ERA for the month. Beck posted seven saves and a 1.46 ERA in July. "One of the big reasons for our consistency is that we have two stoppers in Burky and Billy who keep us from falling into a long losing streak," Williams observed. "Occasionally, Barry will carry us, but it's basically been a team thing. There just aren't that many holes. We have a lot better balance than we did in 1989."

With Burkett, Swift and Beck doing their thing, the Giants never lost more than three games in a row during the first half. They had never been swept in a series. "Consistency is what it's all about," said McGee, who

Bill Swift earned National League Pitcher of the Month honors, with a 5-1 record and a 2.08 ERA.

returned from the Disabled List to collect 15 hits in 33 at-bats (.455) in July. "It's unique to play so well for so long. The big thing is that most of the guys are playing up to their potential. We're like a fine-tuned car. Guys are picking each other up. It's really a team."

Burkett and Swift certainly were doing their part. They each had 15 victories by the end of July, a first in the Majors since Catfish Hunter and Ken Holtzman did it with the 1973 Oakland A's.

Dave Burba went 3-0 in July to help the injured pitching rotation.

GAME OF THE MONTH

During an eight-game stretch that concluded the first half, the Giants scored 74 runs—including a shutout loss in Montreal—and set a club record with six double-digit outbursts.

The 1993 Giants' eminence as an outstanding offensive team was exemplified in the four-game series with the East-leading Philadelphia Phillies at Veterans Stadium, July 8-11. Their three victories were by scores of 13-2, 15-8 and 10-2. The highlight was a season-best 23-hit outburst, July 9, in which the Giants built a 13-0 lead after three innings and coasted 15-8.

Dusty Baker enjoyed life at the top of the Western Division.

"I haven't seen anything like it in a long time, not since the [Cincinnati] Big Red Machine of the 1970s," Manager Dusty Baker said of the week-long eruption. A four-run first featuring Royce Clayton's two-run double got things going in that record romp, July 9. The Giants then sent 11 batters to the plate for seven hits and seven runs in the second inning.

There were no cheapies. Steve Scarsone, a third base replacement for Matt Williams, triggered the explosion with a two-run homer. Will Clark followed with a homer and Barry Bonds, Kirt Manwaring and Paul Faries doubled in the big inning.

When it finally concluded, the Giants had four-hit performances by Scarsone and Manwaring. When the series ended, the Giants had 68 hits and 41 runs, batting .398. "They're in sync," Phillies center fielder Lenny Dykstra said of the Giants. "They have good chemistry."

"I don't need an All-Star break," said Scarsone, who made the most of his rare playing opportunity with a 10-for-20 series and seven RBI. Manwaring batted .529, 9-for-17. Clayton had eight RBI. Bonds had 16 total bases and nine RBI.

"It's beautiful, isn't it?" Baker said as the first half concluded with an 8-5 trip. "Give me a healthy team down the stretch and I'll take my chances."

Steve Scarsone (TOP) started things off with a two-run homer; Will Clark (BOTTOM) followed with a dinger of his own.

Paul Faries filled in for an injured Robby Thompson and helped out offensively with a double.

Rookie lefthander Kevin Rogers earned his first Major League victory in August.

CHAPTER NINE

Down . . . But Not Out!

BY THE NUMBERS
August Standouts
Record: 15-11,
three-and-a-half game lead.

Batting leaders:
Thompson, .394, 39 hits, 8 HR, 23 runs, 18 RBI.
Bonds, .353, 8 HR, 24 runs, 19 RBI.
Williams, .312, 8 2B, 23 runs.

Pitching leaders:
Burkett, 3-2.
Beck, 7 saves, sets record.

Outstanding performances:
Thompson, HRs in 5 consecutive games.
Clark, HR, 3B, 6 RBI at San Diego, 8/3.
Bonds and Williams, back-to-back homers twice, 8/15.
Bonds, 4 hits, 2 HRs, 4 RBI at Pittsburgh, 8/18.
Bonds, four-for-four, HR at Atlanta, 8/31.
Torres wins his Major League debut at Florida, 8/29.

The Giants' erratic August gave a hint of what was to come down the stretch, when the club finally encountered the slump that had been predicted all along. After four months of near-impossible consistency, the Giants finally showed a more human side during a 15-11 August—the first frustrating moments of the 1993 campaign.

Really, there were two Augusts. In the first, the Giants went 7-3 and dual aces John Burkett and Bill Swift continued their winning ways. Then came a three-week struggle in which the stoppers stopped winning, and the relentless Braves made their move.

Against the Reds on Aug. 10-11, Burkett improved to 18-4 with a four-hit, 6-0 victory. Swift improved to 17-5 the next day with a 2-1 triumph. At that point, the prolific pair was a combined 35-9, Rod Beck had the club saves record and the Giants were sailing.

Shortly thereafter, though, Trevor Wilson reinjured himself, and the Giants suddenly had three starters short-circuited. The weakness was disguised during a 4-2 trip to Chicago and Pittsburgh, which featured out-

Scott Sanderson, acquired in early August, played a key role with the Giants down the stretch drive.

standing performances at Wrigley Field, August 15.

On that Sunday afternoon, a crowd of 37,936 watched Robby Thompson single with one out in the third inning for his 1,000th Major League hit. He didn't have time to savor the moment because Barry Bonds and Matt Williams followed with back-to-back homers for a 5-4 Giants' lead. Willie McGee's ninth-inning homer created a 7-6 lead, but the Cubs tied it in the bottom half to preface a rare power burst by the Giants in the top of the 11th.

Facing Randy Myers, who was to set a National League saves record with 53 in 1993, on the mound, Bonds and Williams did it again. This time Bonds hit a 386-foot homer to dead center and Williams followed with a 398-foot bolt over the right field wall. Back-to-back home runs by the same players twice in the same game were a Major League first for 1993, and they rewarded rookie left-

Matt Williams and Barry Bonds helped the Giants' cause on August 15 by hitting two sets of back-to-back homers.

STEPHEN GREEN

Todd Benzinger filled in for Will Clark at first base in late August and early September; he hit .306 (15-for-49) with five home runs in 13 games.

hander Kevin Rogers with his first Major League victory.

With the Braves in hot pursuit, the Giants returned home to win two out of three from the Marlins—the last game on a dramatic ninth-inning homer by Thompson, who was streaking along with five home runs in five consecutive games. Then the Braves came to Candlestick Park, August 23-25, trailing by seven-and-a-half games. A three-game sweep, 5-3, 6-4, and 9-1, left the Giants still four-and-a-half games ahead but desperately seeking pitching help.

They embarked for Miami, Atlanta and St. Louis, now questioning their ability to hold off the Braves. A 7-4

Greg Maddux, a member of the Braves' outstanding pitching rotation, stumped the Giants at home in August.

The Braves felt that Justice was served in San Francisco, as they swept a three-game series against the Giants, August 23-25.

defeat against the Marlins, August 27, made it a season-worst four-game losing streak as Orestes Destrade homered twice and drove in six runs. That's when rookie Salomon Torres, fresh from success at Triple-A Phoenix, provided temporary relief. His debut consisted of seven strong innings and a 9-3 romp over the Marlins, August 29. Todd Benzinger provided a three-run homer.

"I expected to win," the confident Torres said of his long-anticipated maiden start. Added catcher Kirt Manwaring: "I've caught a lot of young pitchers, and he's a cut above." Benzinger hit two more home runs as the injured Will Clark's replacement and Scott Sanderson pitched a 5-1 victory for a two-game winning streak entering a showdown

Salomon Torres made his Major League debut in August.

series at Fulton County Stadium.

Bonds was realistic about the big showdown in light of the Giants' crippled state. "We've got shotguns and they've got Uzis," he said of the Atlanta series. "That just means we can't afford to miss." With Greg Maddux pitching a six-hitter and David Justice providing a two-run homer, the Braves took the opener 8-2 before 46,493. They pulled to within three-and-a-half games of the Giants, who concluded August clinging for their lives.

The Giants actually didn't have a bad month while the problems increased. Bonds batted .353 with eight home runs. Thompson enjoyed a career month with 39 hits, a .394 average, eight home runs and a .727 slugging percentage. But pitching was the sore spot as injuries began to take their toll. The staff yielded 48 home runs in 234-and-two-thirds innings during the month, posting a 4.56 ERA.

Baker, as had become his custom, preferred to look at the bright side. "Any team would take 15-11 as its worst month," he said. "Many teams would take 15-11 as their best month."

It was irrefutable logic, yet the performance level waned during the Giants' first "average" month of the season. The club had spoiled everyone with its exemplary play throughout the first four months—and now it was going to be a tough challenge for the Giants once again to find themselves in a tight pennant race.

GAME OF THE MONTH

Other games may have been more important, but none elicited emotion and provided drama like the August 22 contest with the Florida Marlins at Candlestick Park.

Games with expansion teams normally don't generate much excitement, and there wasn't much to cheer about early in this one as Florida's Pat Rapp, unprotected by the Giants in the expansion draft, enjoyed a 5-2 lead in the seventh inning. Jeff Conine's eighth-inning homer made it 6-2 before the Giants made it interesting and memorable for those among 44,217 paying customers who elected to stick it out.

With one out in the bottom of the eighth and Luis Aquino pitching, Robby Thompson walked and Will Clark singled to left. Matt Williams singled to center, loading the bases. Florida relief ace Bryan Harvey replaced Aquino, and Barry Bonds hit a sacrifice fly for the second out. All the runners advanced on the play, and Willie McGee followed with a two-run single to right, trimming the Marlins' lead to 6-5.

After Kevin Rogers pitched a scoreless ninth, the Giants went back to work off Harvey. Pinch-hitters Todd Benzinger and Mark Carreon were out, but Dave Martinez kept it going with a walk and stole second base.

Thompson, a come-through performer all season, ripped a home run to left, giving the Giants a 7-6 victory and sending the crowd and his teammates into a frenzy. Euphoric teammates mobbed Thompson at the plate in a scene reminiscent of something far more important than a game with an expansion club. But with the Braves coming to town, the Giants definitely needed a lift, and Thompson provided it.

"My heart is still racing," Thompson said long after the home plate celebration. "To win in the last inning like that, and knowing it's a big ballgame...you can't always be cool and collected.

"We showed a little emotion, and it felt great."

Florida had built its early lead with help from first baseman Orestes Destrade's 15th home run.

Dave Martinez got the ninth inning rolling with a walk and a stolen base.

Robby Thompson hit a ninth-inning, two-out, two-run homer to give the Giants one of their most dramatic come-from-behind victories of 1993.

Bill Swift returned to his winning ways in mid-September.

High Anxiety

If August had seen the Giants hit their first few bumps of the 1993 season, September was nothing less than a wild roller-coaster trip—a thrill ride that plunged to the depths of despair, rose to dazzling heights and ended with a lump in the throat.

Within a span of 30 agonizing and thrilling days, the Giants staged a stunning desperation victory in Atlanta, suffered through their worst homestand ever, fell behind the charging Braves and staged a compelling comeback for a frantic finish.

It all began with pinch-hitter John Patterson's game-winning, ninth-inning home run at Fulton County Stadium, September 1, restoring the Giants' lead to four-and-a-half games and temporarily stalling the Braves' bid to overtake them. Atlanta won the final regular-season game between the clubs 5-3 by overcoming a 3-0 Giants' lead off Steve Avery, cutting the lead to three-and-a-half games.

There was a recovery in St. Louis when Jim Deshaies won his Giants' debut 6-1 with six strong innings. Salomon Torres made it two in a row with eight innings and a 3-1 victory. The bullpen squandered Bill Swift's 5-

Pitchers Scott Sanderson (RIGHT) and Salomon Torres (LEFT), along with Jim DeShaies, helped a tired starting rotation.

2 lead in the series finale, but Manager Dusty Baker seemed content heading home with a 5-4 record and the Pirates, Cardinals and Cubs looming just over the horizon.

Scott Sanderson won the homestand opener on Labor Day, beating the Pirates 4-1 with six shutout innings. It seemed like the Giants might have enough energy left to discourage the Braves. John Burkett and Swift had yet to resume their winning ways, but Sanderson, Torres and Deshaies were a combined 6-0 at one stretch, and Baker was looking for the offense to provide some spark despite Will Clark's extended absence.

Instead, the Giants stumbled through an eight-game losing streak, the worst in San Francisco history, and dropped out of first place after 123 consecutive days atop the division. A loss to the Pirates started it. Then the Cardinals posted their first

Will Clark battled through adversity and delivered clutch hits down the stretch.

The winning continued, as Billy Swift (TOP) and John Burkett (PAGE 106) each posted his 20th victory.

four-game sweep of the Giants any-where since 1957 at the Polo Grounds. The Cubs' first three-game sweep at Candlestick since 1977 punctuated a 1-8 homestand.

Everywhere, the feeling was one of stunned disbelief. "We need to get away from here," a disconsolate Barry Bonds said. "This homestand has been like a nightmare. It's been real weird around here lately."

Indeed, the Giants hadn't lost eight in a row at home since June 3-11, 1972. They hadn't endured more losses in a homestand since they went 2-11 earlier in the 1972 season. During the losing streak, they batted .218, averaged 2.4 runs and posted a 5.13 ERA. "Out of control is an understatement," Manager Dusty Baker said. "Everything that can go wrong has gone wrong. It can't get any worse."

Bonds, who had carried the Giants much of the season, now found himself criticized for a lack of run production during the losing streak. When the homestand ended, September 15, he had one home run and one RBI for the month. "What more can Barry do?" Baker asked. "He's done everything we've asked all season. Where would we be without him?"

Robby Thompson agreed, adding: "We're not slumping because of one or two guys—we're slumping as a team." Yet, if the Giants departed

Manager Dusty Baker (TOP), and outfielder Barry Bonds (RIGHT) couldn't hide their disappointment as the Giants went on an eight-game losing skid.

John Burkett

Late in the season, Matt Williams (TOP), and Todd Benzinger (PAGE 108) joined the hit parade.

Candlestick in a state of depression, they didn't show it. There was an off-day team party in Cincinnati. Relaxed and resolved, the Giants began to demonstrate the character that made the 1993 team so special.

The slump concluded convincingly with a 13-0 romp over the Reds behind Swift's shutout pitching. Kirt Manwaring had four hits and Matt Williams homered, his career-high 35th. "It's a big relief," Baker said. "I hope it won't take as long to get to 100 victories as it did to get to 90." Todd Benzinger homered twice and Burkett pitched a 6-1 victory the next day. Then Williams hit a pair of

400-foot homers to dead center—his ninth and 10th in 15 games—for a 7-3 victory and a three-game sweep.

"I'm getting good counts, and that's the key," Williams said of his slugging spree. "This is a good groove, but my home runs have always come in streaks." Added Baker: "We needed a sweep, and we got one. We're starting to feel good about ourselves again. Matt hasn't just stepped forward; he's jumped forward."

The Giants finished 11-2 against the Reds, their best record ever against Cincinnati. But the big news over their weekend was that the slump was history, for the team and

for win-starved aces Burkett and Swift.

Collectively, they had gone 0-6 with a 7.04 ERA in their previous 11 starts. When they posted back-to-back victories in early August, the team enjoyed a nine-game lead. The Giants were four games behind when they finally won again in Cincinnati.

They wouldn't lose again. The Giants won three out of four at the Astrodome for a redeeming 6-1 trip under extreme pressure. Swift pitched eight shutout innings against the Astros to improve to 19-8. "This is the best I've felt all year," said Swift, who was a winner on Willie McGee's bunt and Manwaring's double off Pete Harnisch in the seventh. "I've caught my second wind."

The next night, Burkett became the Giants' first 20-game winner since Mike Krukow in 1986. He retired the last 13 batters in eight shutout innings. Bonds powered a 12-hit attack with three doubles. "This trip showed what these guys are made of," Burkett said. "When I said in Spring Training that I could win 20, I was thinking of all the runs I would get. This game was typical."

Baker was beaming. The Braves' lead was slashed to two-and-a-half games with 10 to go. He praised the players for not succumbing mentally or physically following the 1-8 homestand. "A lot of people had us counted out," the manager said. "But all that matters is what we think. To the players, [a division title] is very reachable."

The Giants returned to sweep four games from the Padres, a series that featured four Bonds home runs, a dramatic game-winning homer by Will Clark and Swift's 20th victory. Clark, in his second game back from a knee injury, was The Thrill once again in the homestand opener, September 24. With the Padres leading 3-2 in the eighth inning, Thompson had his left cheekbone fractured by a Trevor Hoffman fast-ball. Mike Benjamin ran for Thompson and went to third on Clark's single. Williams' sacrifice fly produced a tie. With two outs in the bottom of the 10th, Clark's off-field homer produced a 4-3 victory and a wild celebration. Victories by Swift and Burkett completed the sweep of San Diego, Swifty yielding three hits over eight innings to improve to 20-8 with a 5-2 triumph, September 26.

Bryan Hickerson's 6-4 victory over the Rockies the next night coupled with the Braves' loss to Houston created a tie. But two Daryl Boston homers helped Colorado to a 5-3 victory over Torres in the home finale, once again dropping the Giants to second. The Giants announced a record home attendance of 2,606,354, but that was the only good news. The loss made the Giants realize their task in the final four-game series at Los Angeles would be more difficult. "We've got to win all four now," Bonds said as the Giants packed for their final trip.

It began on a positive note. Swift yielded two hits over seven innings and improved to 21-8 with a 3-1 victory over the Dodgers. The Astros defeated the Braves again, producing a dead heat at 101-58 with three weekend games remaining. The Giants thereby concluded a 16-12 September with high hopes intact. Their confidence was restored with 12 victories in 14 games following the horrid slump. Suddenly, there was brightness instead of gloom.

GAME OF THE MONTH

Clark's game-winning home run against the Padres cannot be minimized, yet it paled in comparison to the significance of what transpired at Fulton County Stadium, September 1. A crowd of 49,290 gathered to watch the Braves continue their march toward a third consecutive division championship. In a span of nine days, they'd won four in a row from the Giants to slice the lead to three-and-a-half games.

The tension was thick, as Bryan Hickerson started against John Smoltz in the second game of the final series between the two contenders. There was no score after three innings. Fred McGriff's two-out walk, Hickerson's wild pitch and Terry Pendleton's single made it 1-0 in the fourth. Willie McGee's two-out double and Matt Williams' single created a tie in the fifth. Atlanta answered in the sixth when Otis Nixon led off with a single, stole second and scored on Jeff Blauser's double. Jeff Reed's double, Mike Benjamin's sacrifice and Dave Martinez' single made it 2-2 in the seventh.

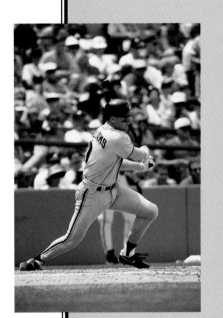

Matt Williams hit a key single to knock in Willie McGee and create a tie in the fifth inning.

Kevin Rogers pulled Hickerson out of further trouble in the sixth and retired the side in the seventh. Braves reliever Mark Wohlers and the Giants' Mike Jackson did likewise in the eighth, keeping the game deadlocked entering the ninth inning.

Patterson, whose shoulder problems restricted him to 16 games at Class-A San Jose, was summoned to bat for Jackson as the leadoff hitter in the ninth. It was his first Major League at-bat of the season, and it was a gem. Patterson made the most of his moment by drilling a 2-0 fastball far over the right field fence for a 3-2 Giants' lead that held up while Rod Beck worked a one-two-three ninth. The Braves would not sweep.

"We called in the cavalry," Manager Dusty Baker said after his hunch on using Patterson, his last remaining left-handed hitter on the bench, paid off handsomely. "We've had some clutch hits this season, but none were bigger than John's."

Indeed, it truly was a shot in the dark. Not only was Patterson an unlikely home run hero, but the right-handed Wohlers had not yielded a homer in exactly two years and 71 games. "It's my biggest thrill in baseball," Patterson said. "The guys on the bench told me to look for a fastball, and I did. I was thinking it was a good time to get a big hit."

Kirt Manwaring protected the plate against scoring Braves.

Pinch-hitter John Patterson hit a game-winning homer in Atlanta in his first Major League at-bat of 1993.

The Giants celebrated their 3-1 victory over the Dodgers on September 30, and looked ahead to a rough October.

CHAPTER ELEVEN

Heartbreak and Heroics

BY THE NUMBERS
Down to the Wire
Record: 2-1, one game behind

Batting leaders:
Clark, 9-for-16, 5 runs in 3 games.
Williams, 6-for-14 in 3 games.

Pitching leaders:
Burkett's 22nd win at L.A.
Brantley's first win since 6/20.

Outstanding performances:
Bonds' career-high 7 RBI at L.A., 10/1.
Clark's back-to-back four-hit games.
Martinez' game-winning double, 10/2.

Ghosts of the Giants and Dodgers storied rivalry showed up at Dodgers Stadium on the final weekend of the season—and it wasn't even yet Halloween. There was 1951 home run hero Bobby Thomson sitting with Managing General Partner Peter Magowan. Willie Mays made the trip to add inspiration to the Giants' crucial mission. And 1982 Dodger-killer Joe Morgan was on hand in the broadcast booth.

With the Atlanta Braves hosting the expansion Colorado Rockies, it didn't seem likely there would be much margin for error as the Giants entered October in a first-place tie.

The atmosphere was pressure-packed, as it had been in 1951 when Thomson gave the Giants the pennant over Brooklyn with his historic playoff home run off the Dodgers' Ralph Branca. It was reminiscent of 1962, when the Giants had caught the Dodgers on the final day and gone on to win a Game 3 playoff with a four-run ninth at Dodger Stadium to win the pennant.

The Dodgers, for their part, were reminded of Joe Morgan's home run off Terry Forster in 1982, eliminating the Dodgers again. And of Trevor Wilson's final-weekend 1991 victory over L.A., which made Atlanta the champion.

History was a prominent part of the final weekend, but it meant little to

After throwing a no-hitter against San Francisco in 1992, veteran pitcher Kevin Gross (LEFT) stumped the Giants' rookie, Salomon Torres (RIGHT.)

the players who were far more concerned with their performance on the field than with dwelling on tradition.

With the Braves posting a 7-4 victory, the Giants were under pressure to keep pace on October 1. It didn't look good when the Dodgers jumped on John Burkett for a 4-0 lead after two innings. But Darren Lewis' triple and Will Clark's one-out double off Ramon Martinez got the Giants going in the third. Matt Williams followed

with a single and Barry Bonds' three-run homer made it 4-4.

Clark opened the fifth with a single and went to third on Williams' double, chasing Martinez. Omar Daal took over and was greeted by Bonds' second three-run homer of the game for a 7-4 lead en route to an 8-7 victory. "It's a two-game season now," Bonds said after blasting his 45th and 46th homers and finishing with a career-high seven RBI. "They

Dave Martinez, filling in for an injured McGee, batted in the tying and go-ahead runs in the Giants' 5-2 win over Los Angeles on October 2.

Giants fans made a pilgrimage to Los Angeles to cheer on their team.

Long-time nemesis Orel Hershiser couldn't knock the Giants out of first place on October 2.

National League Rookie of the Year Mike Piazza shined for the Dodgers on October 3 with spectacular defense and two home runs.

[Dodgers] came out firing, so we had to turn it around."

The Giants entered the October 2 game still tied, and they couldn't relax while the Braves were demolishing the Rockies 10-1. It would take another victory to maintain the tie, and the task was entrusted to Bryan Hickerson.

Given a 2-0 lead in the second inning, he couldn't hold it. The Dodgers scored in the second inning and chased him before scoring the tying run in the third. But Jeff Brantley, winless since June 20,

blanked the Dodgers over four innings while the Giants pecked away at long-time nemesis Orel Hershiser. Clark's double and a run-scoring grounder by Dave Martinez broke the tie in the fifth. Clark led off the seventh with a single and advanced on a long fly. Bonds was walked intentionally. Martinez then lined a 2-1 pitch to center for a two-run double and a 5-2 lead. Brantley had his win and Rod Beck worked a scoreless ninth for his 48th save.

It would come down to the final

Dusty Baker called for pitching reinforcements as dejected players looked on.

On October 2, working in his sixth straight game, Rod Beck recorded his 48th save.

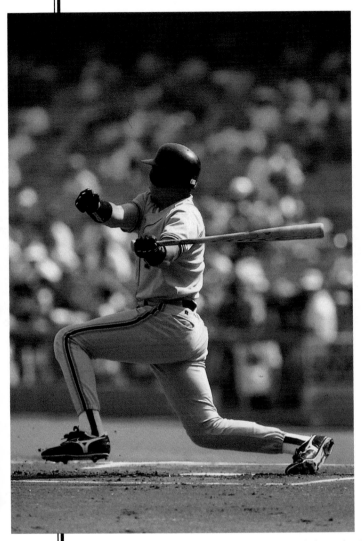

Lewis (LEFT) and Clark (RIGHT) were a great help to the Giants' October expedition.

day, and it was perceived as a good omen because the season would be decided on October 3rd—the same day on which Thomson and Morgan had struck down the Dodgers with home runs, and the same day as the 1962 pennant clincher in L.A.

But this time, the Giants didn't rise to the occasion, picking the wrong time to have one of their worst games. After the Braves downed the Rockies to clinch a tie, the Dodgers demolished the Giants 12-1 behind rookie Mike Piazza's two home runs and Kevin Gross' pitching.

There would be no one-game play-off the next night at Candlestick Park. There would be no NLCS or World Series. The Giants were going home with broken hearts and memories of a brilliant season. "That's life," Baker summed up. "The guys gave me all they had. I told them to walk proud and with their heads high. They had a great season. They just fell one game short."

Robby Thompson courageously started the Giants' final game of the season in L.A., just eight days after an errant pitch fractured his left cheekbone.

Bobby Thomson, who hit the "Shot Heard 'Round the World" in 1951, attended the Giants' final series in Los Angeles.

Dusty Baker told reporters that his players should hold their heads high after their great season.

GAME OF THE MONTH

Barry Bonds' punctuation mark on a career year made the first game of October memorable, while giving a clue of what might have been had Will Clark enjoyed a more-typical season.

With the Giants requiring a victory to stay tied with the Atlanta Braves, the heart of the Giants' batting order combined for 10 hits in 13 at-bats, 19 total bases, seven runs and eight RBI in an 8-7 victory at Dodger Stadium.

Bonds had seven of those RBI with a pair of three-run homers and a run-scoring double as the Giants overcame a 4-0 deficit after the first two innings to hand John Burkett his 22nd victory. "My adrenaline was so high, my fingers were aching," Bonds said of his dynamic day. "This was big to me because we needed a win and because it's the Giants-Dodgers."

The RBI binge gave Bonds a total of 123 and the National League RBI lead. His two homers gave him a league-leading 46 and seven multiple-homer games for the season. "It means a lot when Will can set the table," Bonds said of Clark, who had his first four-hit game of the season and scored three runs.

Rod Beck added some drama to the ninth inning by allowing an Eric Karros homer, but finished off the Dodgers for an 8-7 victory.

Clark, who added four more hits the next day, was fired up by his sizzling final weekend. "I'm a little more juiced now," he said. "I didn't come down here to lose." A crowd of 51,860, many of them rooting for the Giants, watched Bonds' seventh-inning double make it 8-4. It turned out to be the winning run because of a Dodgers' comeback against a weary bullpen.

Dave Hansen homered off Dave Burba in the bottom of the seventh. Rod Beck struck out Jose Offerman to end the eighth inning, but created anxious moments in the bottom of the ninth. Hansen's single and Eric Karros' homer made it a one-run game, but Beck rebounded to strike out Henry Rodriguez and to retire Cory Snyder on a fly to right, ending the game and keeping the Giants alive for a memorable last-day showdown.

John Burkett won the October 1 game in Los Angeles, with offensive help from his teammates.

Barry Bonds had an amazing seven RBI with two three-run homers on the first game of October against the Dodgers.

Will Clark (LEFT) rose to the occasion in L.A. with four hits and three runs; he was then congratulated by teammate Barry Bonds.

The Record

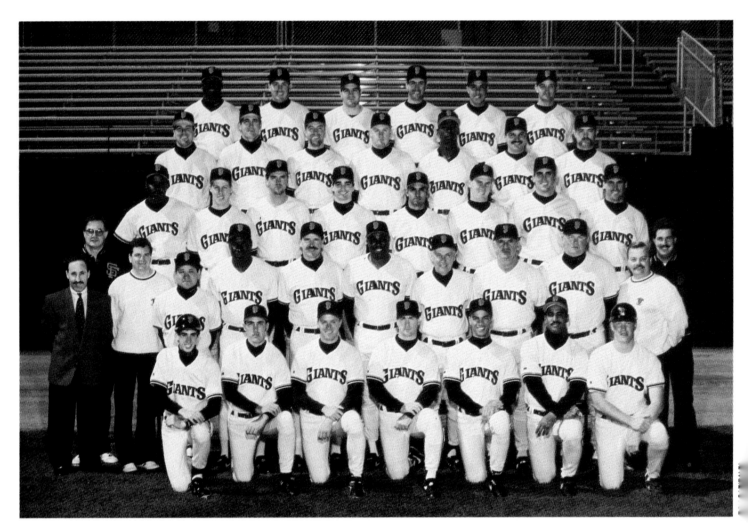

The 1993 San Francisco Giants.

CHAPTER TWELVE

The Greatest Team of All?

More than three decades later, memories of the magical 1962 season still haven't lost their luster.

It was the year of Mays, McCovey, Marichal and Cepeda, when the Giants finally overcame all odds and pushed to a first-place tie atop the National League standings on the last day of the season. Then, after a tense three-game playoff series against the rival Dodgers, San Francisco's team emerged as the National League's best for the first time ever.

It seems obvious then the summer of '62 would continue to hold the most sacred spot in the hearts of Giants fans—the San Francisco Giants' finest season. But was it? Whereas the 1962 powerhouse made it to the World Series, a compelling argument could be made that the 1993 Giants were, in fact, the best team to wear San Francisco uniforms. After all, the '93 boys of summer

Despite being tagged out at home, Willie Mays and the Giants stayed alive in the '62 National League pennant race.

enjoyed a better regular-season record—at 103-59 the best in San Francisco history—despite running into an Atlanta Braves' buzzsaw that posted a franchise-record 104 victories.

Like the most recent Giants, the 1962 squad displayed excellent balance in a record-breaking season,

The middlemen—Clark, Williams and Bonds—helped the Giants offense.

The 1993 Giants improved by 31 games over their 1992 record.

combining power at the plate with stout pitching, as key ingredients for success. With Felipe Alou (.316), Orlando Cepeda (.306), Willie Mays (.304), Harvey Kuenn (.304) and Jim Davenport (.297) having great years, the 1962 team led the league with a .278 average, a San Francisco record. But right behind them on the S.F. all-time list are Barry Bonds (.336), Robby Thompson (.312), Willie McGee (.301) and Matt Williams (.294), who carried the load for a league-leading .276 average in 1993.

Mays (49 homers, 141 RBI) and Cepeda (35 HR, 114 RBI) provided much of the power in 1962, combining for 339 home runs and RBI. Bonds (46-123) and Williams (38-110) slugged their way to a 317 total in 1993. Each team also topped the league in home runs, aided by a strong bench.

The 1962 champions, like last summer's Giants, had strong hitting throughout the lineup. Alou con-

The 1962 San Francisco Giants.

tributed 25 homers and 98 RBI. The catching platoon of Tom Haller and Ed Bailey provided 35 home runs and 100 RBI. Mays led the league with 49 home runs in 1962. Bonds, his godson, did likewise with 46 last season. "Bonds is very Mays-like," said Felipe Alou, now manager of the Montreal Expos.

There can be no argument that the 1962 team had stronger starting pitching with Jack Sanford (24-7), Billy O'Dell (19-14), Juan Marichal (18-11) and Billy Pierce (16-6) combining for 77 victories. However, John Burkett (22-7) and Bill Swift (21-8) were a formidable one-two punch in 1993, and their bullpen was much better with Rod Beck posting a franchise-record 48 saves.

The 1993 club also was much better defensively, setting a franchise record for fewest errors (101) and fielding percentage (.984) while being expert at turning the double play. And whereas Alvin Darks' 1962 club stumbled down the stretch (7-6) to catch the reeling Dodgers (3-10) on the final day, the 1993 Giants went 14-3 at the finish and fell just short of the prize.

So, what does it all mean? Would Marichal whip fastballs past the Clark-Williams-Bonds lineup? Would Mays or McCovey solve a Bill Swift sinker or beat out a strong-throwing Kirt Manwaring on the steal? It's an argument—and a game—that can be played out only in the imagination. But that's what most compellingly links both teams—each had the ability to accumulate victories and to excite the imagination of an entire community with inspired performances.

WHO'S THE GREATEST?

Here's a comparison of the 1993 and 1962 Giants—the only two San Francisco teams to post winning records every month:

	1962	1993
Won-Lost	103-62	103-59
Home	61-21	50-31
Road	42-41	53-28

BATTING

	1962	1993
Batting	.278*	.276*
Runs	878*	808
Hits	1552*	1534
Doubles	235	269
Triples	32	33
Homers	204*	168
Walks	523	516
Strikeouts	822	930
Slugging	.441*	.427*
On-base	.334*	.340
Steals	73	120

FIELDING

	1962	1993
Errors	142	101*
DPs	153	169*
Fielding	.977	.984*

PITCHING

	1962	1993
ERA	3.79	3.61
Complete	62*	4
Shutouts	10	9
Saves	39	50
Innings	1462	1457
Hits	1399	1385
Strikeouts	886	982
Walks	503	442

*Led league

MONTHLY RECORDS

	1962	1993
April	15-5	15-9
May	20-10	18-9
June	16-13	19-9
Before All-Star break	57-31	59-30
July	16-11	18-8
August	18-10	15-11
September	16-12	16-12
October	2-1	2-1
After All-Star break	52-34	51-32

Willie McCovey (LEFT), Juan Marichal (RIGHT), Willie Mays (PAGE 133 LEFT) and Orlando Cepeda (PAGE 133 RIGHT) helped make the 1962 squad one of the greatest Giants' teams of all time.

1993
Day-by-Day Record

#	DATE	D/N	OPP	WINNER/LOSER	W/L	SCORE	RECORD	POS	GB	CLUB
1	4/6	N	at STL	Burkett (1-0)/Tewksbury	W	2-1	1-0	T1	-	CIN
2	4/7	N	at STL	Cormier/Wilson (0-1)	L	2-6	1-1	T3	-0.5	ATL/LA
3	4/8	D	at STL	Osborne/Rogers (0-1)	L	1-2	1-2	T3	-1.5	ATL
4	4/9	N	at PIT	Minor/ Beck (0-1)	L	5-6	1-3	T5	-2.5	ATL
5	4/10	D	at PIT	Burba (1-0)/Cooke	W	12-5	2-3	T4	-1.5	ATL
6	4/11	D	at PIT	Burkett (2-0)/Wakefield	W	4-3	3-3	T2	-0.5	ATL
7	4/12	D	FLA	Beck (1-1)/Klink	W	4-3 (11)	4-3	T2	-1.5	ATL
8	4/13	D	FLA	Burba (2-0)/Aquino	W	3-1	5-3	2	-0.5	ATL
9	4/14	D	FLA	Bowen/Swift (0-1)	L	4-6	5-4	3	-0.5	HOU/ATL
10	4/15	N	ATL	Brantley (1-0)/G. Maddux	W	6-1	6-4	1	+0.5	CIN/HOU
11	4/16	N	ATL	Burkett (3-0)/SMOLTZ	W	1-0	7-4	1	+0.5	HOU
12	4/17	D	ATL	Avery/Jackson (0-1)	L	0-2	7-5	1	+0.5	ATL/HOU
13	4/18	D	ATL	Jackson (1-1)/Bedrosian	W	13-12 (11)	8-5	1	+0.5	HOU
-	4/19	OFF DAY						1	+0.5	HOU
14	4/20	N	at N.Y.	Righetti (1-0)/M. Maddux	W	4-1 (11)	9-5	1	+1.5	ATL/HOU
15	4/21	N	at N.Y.	Gooden/Brantley (1-1)	L	0-10	9-6	1	+0.5	ATL/HOU
16	4/22	N	at N.Y.	Burkett (4-0)/Schourek	W	13-4	10-6	1	+1	HOU
17	4/23	N	at MON	Martinez/Wilson (0-2)	L	2-7	10-7	T1	-	HOU
18	4/24	D	at MON	HILL/Burba (2-1)	L	1-6	10-8	3	-1	HOU
19	4/25	D	at MON	Swift (1-1)/Nabholz	W	4-1	11-8	T1	-	HOU
20	4/26	N	at PHI	Andersen/Minutelli (0-1)	L	8-9 (10)	11-9	T1	-	HOU

21	4/27	D	at PHI	Burkett (5-0)/Mulholland	W	6-3	12-9	T1	-	HOU
22	4/28	N	N.Y.	Beck (2-1)/Innis	W	4-3	13-9	T1	-	HOU
23	4/29	D	N.Y.	Black (1-0)/Saberhagen	W	10-5	14-9	T1	-	HOU
24	4/30	N	MON	Swift (2-1)/Nabholz	W	5-2	15-9	T1	-	HOU
25	5/1	D	MON	Brantley (2-1)/J. Jones	W	7-3	16-9	T1	-	HOU
26	5/2	D	MON	Jackson (2-1)/Fassero	W	4-3 (11)	17-9	1	+1.0	HOU
-	5/3	OFF DAY						1	+1.0	HOU
27	5/4	N	PHI	Andersen/Righetti (1-1)	L	3-4 (12)	17-10	1	+1.0	HOU
28	5/5	D	PHI	Swift (3-1)/D. Jackson	W	11-2	18-10	1	+1.0	HOU
-	5/6	OFF DAY						1	+1.5	HOU
29	5/7	N	L.A.	Black (2-0)/Gross	W	8-5	19-10	1	+2.5	HOU
30	5/8	D	L.A.	Gott/Burba (2-2)	L	2-5 (12)	19-11	1	+1.5	HOU
31	5/9	D	L.A.	Hershiser/Brantley (2-2)	L	4-7	19-12	1	+0.5	HOU
32	5/10	N	at COL	REYNOSO/Wilson (0-3)	L	4-7	19-13	2	-0.5	HOU
33	5/11	N	at COL	Swift (4-1)/Nied	W	5-3	20-13	1	+0.5	HOU
34	5/12	N	at COL	Black (3-0)/Henry	W	8-2	21-13	1	+1.5	HOU
35	5/13	D	at COL	Burkett (6-0)/Ruffin	W	13-8	22-13	1	+2.0	HOU
36	5/14	N	at S.D.	GR. HARRIS/Brantley (2-3)	L	1-3	22-14	1	+1.0	HOU
37	5/15	N	at S.D.	Wilson (1-3)/Taylor	W	3-0	23-14	1	+1.0	HOU
38	5/16	N	at S.D.	Swift (5-1)/Whitehurst	W	9-4	24-14	1	+1.0	HOU
39	5/17	D	HOU	Burba (3-2)/D. Jones	W	8-7 (10)	25-14	1	+2.0	HOU
40	5/18	N	HOU	BURKETT (7-0)/Kile	W	7-2	26-14	1	+3.0	HOU
41	5/19	D	HOU	Brantley (3-3)/Harnisch	W	6-3	27-14	1	+3.5	ATL
42	5/20	D	CIN	Wilson (2-3)/Browning	W	6-1	28-14	1	+4.0	ATL
43	5/21	N	CIN	Swift (6-1)/Belcher	W	3-0	29-14	1	+4.0	ATL
44	5/22	D	CIN	Rijo/Black (3-1)	L	2-6	29-15	T1	+4.0	ATL
45	5/23	D	CIN	Jackson (3-1)/Landrum	W	4-3	30-15	1	+4.0	ATL
-	5/24	OFF DAY						1	+4.0	ATL
46	5/25	D	at CHI	Burba (4-2)/Myers	W	5-4	31-15	1	+4.0	ATL
47	5/26	D	at CHI	Harkey/Swift (6-2)	L	2-4	31-16	1	+4.0	ATL
48	5/27	N	at CHI	Hibbard/Hickerson (0-1)	L	4-5	31-17	1	+4.0	ATL
49	5/28	N	at ATL	Avery/Burkett (7-1)	L	4-7	31-18	1	+3.0	ATL
50	5/29	D	at ATL	Brummett (1-0)/P. Smith	W	6-3	32-18	1	+4.0	ATL
51	5/30	D	at ATL	Burba (5-2)/Glavine	W	4-3	33-18	1	+5.0	ATL
-	5/31	RAINED OUT						1	+4.5	ATL
52	6/1	D	at FLA	Hammond/Swift (6-2)	L	3-7	33-19			

53	DH	N	at FLA	Black (4-1)/Bowen	W	4-3	34-19	1	+5.0	ATL
54	6/2	N	at FLA	Burkett (8-1)/Armstrong	W	3-2	35-19	1	+5.0	ATL
55	6/3	N	PIT	Neagle/Brummett (1-1)	L	1-2	35-20	1	+5.0	ATL/HOU
56	6/4	N	PIT	Cooke/Brantley (3-4)	L	2-3	35-21	1	+4.0	HOU
57	6/5	D	PIT	Wilson (3-3)/Wakefield	W	3-2	36-21	1	+4.0	HOU
58	6/6	D	PIT	Swift (7-3)/Walk	W	7-1	37-21	1	+4.0	HOU
-	6/7	OFF DAY						1	+4.5	HOU
59	6/8	D	STL	Arocha/Burkett (8-2)	L	3-4	37-22	1	+3.5	HOU
60	6/9	D	STL	Black (5-1)/Osborne	W	3-1	38-22	1	+4.5	HOU
-	6/10	OFF DAY						1	+4.5	HOU
61	6/11	N	CHI	WILSON (4-3)/Hibbard	W	7-2	39-22	1	+5.5	HOU
62	6/12	D	CHI	Swift (8-3)/McElroy	W	5-4	40-22	1	+6.5	ATL/HOU
63	6/13	D	CHI	Burkett (9-2)/Morgan	W	5-3	41-22	1	+6.5	ATL
-	6/14	OFF DAY						1	+7.0	ATL/LA
64	6/15	N	at CIN	Belcher/Brantley (3-5)	L	5-10	41-23	1	+6.0	ATL/LA
65	6/16	N	at CIN	Jackson (4-1)/Ayala	W	6-5 (10)	42-23	1	+6.0	ATL
66	6/17	D	at CIN	Swift (9-3)/Smiley	W	5-1	43-23	1	+6.5	ATL
67	6/18	N	at HOU	Black (6-1)/Drabek	W	5-0	44-23	1	+7.5	ATL
68	6/19	N	at HOU	Burkett (10-2)/Swindell	W	10-3	45-23	1	+7.5	ATL
69	6/20	D	at HOU	Brantley (4-5)/Williams	W	8-5	46-23	1	+7.5	ATL
70	6/21	N	S.D.	Wilson (5-3)/Brocail	W	2-1	47-23	1	+7.5	ATL
71	6/22	N	S.D.	Benes/ Swift (9-4)	L	1-2	47-24	1	+7.5	ATL
72	6/23	D	S.D.	Black (7-1)/Gr. Harris	W	6-2	48-24	1	+8.5	ATL
73	6/24	D	COL	Burkett (11-2)/Blair	W	17-2	49-24	1	+9.0	ATL
74	6/25	N	COL	Hickerson (1-1)/Henry	W	7-2	50-24	1	+9.0	ATL
75	6/26	D	COL	REYNOSO/ Wilson (5-4)	L	1-5	50-25	1	+8.0	ATL
76	6/27	D	COL	Swift (10-4)/Leskanic	W	5-0	51-25	1	+9.0	ATL
77	6/28	N	at L.A.	P. Martinez/Jackson (4-2)	L	0-4	51-26	1	+8.5	ATL
78	6/29	N	at L.A.	Burkett (12-2)/Hershiser	W	3-1	52-26	1	+8.5	ATL
79	6/30	N	at L.A.	P. Martinez/Rogers (0-2)	L	3-5	52-27	1	+7.5	ATL
-	7/1	OFF DAY						1	+7.0	ATL
80	7/2	N	at N.Y.	Burba (6-2)/Young	W	3-1	53-27	1	+8.0	ATL
81	7/3	N	at N.Y.	Telgheder/Swift (10-5)	L	3-6	53-28	1	+7.0	ATL
82	7/4	D	at N.Y.	Jackson (5-2)/M. Maddux	W	10-8	54-28	1	+7.0	ATL
83	7/5	N	at MON	Burkett (13-2)/Gardiner	W	10-4	55-28	1	+7.0	ATL
84	7/6	N	at MON	Hickerson (2-1)/Bottenfield	W	13-5	56-28	1	+8.0	ATL

85	7/7	N	at MON	Rueter/Brummett (1-2)	L	0-3	56-29	1	+8.0	ATL
86	7/8	N	at PHI	Swift (11-5)/D. Jackson	W	13-2	57-29	1	+9.0	ATL
87	7/9	N	at PHI	Black (8-1)/Rivera	W	15-8	58-29	1	+9.0	ATL
88	7/10	D	at PHI	Greene/Burkett (13-3)	L	3-8	58-30	1	+9.0	ATL
89	7/11	D	at PHI	Hickerson (3-1)/Schilling	W	10-2	59-30	1	+9.0	ATL

ALL-STAR BREAK RECORD: 59-30

90	7/15	D	N.Y.	Swift (12-5)/Hillman	W	8-1	60-30	1	+9.0	ATL
91	7/16	N	N.Y.	Hickerson (4-0)/GOODEN	W	4-2	61-30	1	+9.0	ATL
92	7/17	D	N.Y.	Tanana/Burkett (13-4)	L	1-3	61-31	1	+9.0	ATL
93	7/18	D	N.Y.	Schourek/Brummett (1-3)	L	6-12	61-32	1	+8.0	ATL
94	7/19	D	MON	Burba (7-2)/Nabholz	W	6-2	62-32	1	+9.0	ATL
95	7/20	D	MON	Swift (13-5)/Martinez	W	8-3	63-32	1	+9.0	ATL
96	7/21	D	MON	Hickerson (5-1)/Rojas	W	4-3	64-32	1	+9.0	ATL
97	7/22	D	PHI	Burkett (14-4)/Mulholland	W	4-1	65-32	1	+10.0	ATL
98	7/23	N	PHI	West/Jackson (5-3)	L	1-2 (13)	65-33	1	+9.0	ATL
99	7/24	D	PHI	Burba (8-2)/Rivera	W	5-4	66-33	1	+9.0	ATL
100	7/25	D	PHI	Swift (14-5)/Jackson	W	5-2	67-33	1	+9.0	ATL
101	7/26	D	L.A.	HERSHISER/Hickerson (5-2)	L	1-15	67-34	1	+8.0	ATL
102	7/27	N	L.A.	Burkett (15-4)/Gross	W	3-2	68-34	1	+8.0	ATL
103	7/28	D	L.A.	Candiotti/Black (8-2)	L	1-2	68-35	1	+7.0	ATL
-	7/29	OFF DAY						1	+7.5	ATL
104	7/30	N	at COL	Brummett (2-3)/Gr. Harris	W	10-4	69-35	1	+7.5	ATL
105	7/31	N	at COL	Swift (15-5)/Bottenfield	W	4-3	70-35	1	+7.5	ATL
106	8/1	D	at COL	Burkett (16-4)/Reynoso	W	6-5	71-35	1	+7.5	ATL
-	8/2	OFF DAY						1	+7.5	ATL
107	8/3	N	at S.D.	Burba (9-2)/M. Davis	W	12-7	72-35	1	+8.5	ATL
108	8/4	N	at S.D.	Pa. Martinez/Hickerson (5-3)	L	10-11 (12)	72-36	1	+7.5	ATL
109	8/5	D	at S.D.	Swift (16-5)/Ashby	W	5-3	73-36	1	+8.5	ATL
110	8/6	N	HOU	Burkett (17-4)/Kile	W	4-3	74-36	1	+9.5	ATL
111	8/7	D	HOU	Swindell/Sanderson (0-1)	L	5-6	74-37	1	+9.5	ATL
112	8/8	D	HOU	Portugal/Hickerson (5-4)	L	1-4	74-38	1	+8.5	ATL
113	8/9	D	CIN	Burba (10-2)/Ruffin	W	10-7	75-38	1	+9.0	ATL
114	8/10	D	CIN	Swift (17-5)/Rijo	W	2-1	76-38	1	+9.0	ATL
115	8/11	D	CIN	BURKETT (18-4)/Ayala	W	6-0	77-38	1	+9.0	ATL
-	8/12	OFF DAY						1	+8.5	ATL

116	8/13	D	at CHI	Wilson (6-4)/Hibbard	W	4-1	78-38	1	+8.5	ATL
117	8/14	D	at CHI	Myers/Jackson (5-4)	L	2-3	78-39	1	+7.5	ATL
118	8/15	D	at CHI	Rogers (1-2)/Myers	W	9-7 (11)	79-39	1	+7.5	ATL
-	8/16	OFF DAY						1	+7.5	ATL
119	8/17	N	at PIT	Cooke/Burkett (18-5)	L	3-10	79-40	1	+6.5	ATL
120	8/18	N	at PIT	Wilson (7-4)/Z. Smith	W	9-6	80-40	1	+6.5	ATL
121	8/19	D	at PIT	Hickerson (6-4)/Walk	W	6-3	81-40	1	+6.5	ATL
122	8/20	N	FLA	Bowen/Jackson (5-5)	L	4-5	81-41	1	+7.5	ATL
123	8/21	D	FLA	Sanderson (1-1)/Hammond	W	7-4	82-41	1	+7.5	ATL
124	8/22	D	FLA	Rogers (2-2)/Harvey	W	7-6	83-41	1	+7.5	ATL
125	8/23	N	ATL	AVERY/Wilson (7-5)	L	3-5	83-42	1	+6.5	ATL
126	8/24	D	ATL	Glavine/Hickerson (6-5)	L	4-6	83-43	1	+5.5	ATL
127	8/25	D	ATL	G. Maddux/Swift (17-6)	L	1-9	83-44	1	+4.5	ATL
-	8/26	OFF DAY						1	+4.5	ATL
128	8/27	N	at FLA	Rapp/Burkett (18-6)	L	4-7	83-45	1	+4.5	ATL
-	8/28	OFF DAY						1	+4.0	ATL
129	8/29	N	at FLA	Torres (1-0)/Hammond	W	9-3	84-45	1	+4.0	ATL
130	8/30	N	at FLA	Sanderson (2-1)/Armstrong	W	5-1	85-45	1	+4.5	ATL
131	8/31	N	at ATL	G. MADDUX/Swift (17-7)	L	2-8	85-46	1	+3.5	ATL
132	9/1	N	at ATL	Jackson (6-5)/Wohlers	W	3-2	86-46	1	+4.5	ATL
133	9/2	N	at ATL	Wohlers/Brantley (4-6)	L	3-5	86-47	1	+3.5	ATL
134	9/3	N	at STL	Deshaies (1-0)/Watson	W	6-1	87-47	1	+3.5	ATL
135	9/4	N	at STL	Torres (2-0)/Arocha	W	3-1	88-47	1	+3.5	ATL
136	9/5	D	at STL	Olivares/Burba (10-3)	L	6-7	88-48	1	+2.5	ATL
137	9/6	D	PIT	Sanderson (3-1)/Wagner	W	4-1	89-48	1	+3.5	ATL
138	9/7	N	PIT	Menendez/Jackson (6-6)	L	3-4	89-49	1	+2.5	ATL
-	9/8	OFF DAY						1	+2.0	ATL
139	9/9	N	STL	Arocha/Deshaies (1-1)	L	4-9	89-50	1	+1.0	ATL
140	9/10	N	STL	Urbani/Torres (2-1)	L	2-6	89-51	1	-	ATL
141	9/11	D	STL	Tewksbury/Swift (17-8)	L	1-3	89-52	2	-1.0	ATL
142	9/12	D	STL	Cormier/Burkett (18-7)	L	2-4	89-53	2	-1.0	ATL
143	9/13	N	CHI	Hibbard/Sanderson (3-2)	L	5-6	89-54	2	-1.5	ATL
144	9/14	N	CHI	BAUTISTA/Deshaies (1-2)	L	1-8	89-55	2	-2.5	ATL
145	9/15	D	CHI	Morgan/Torres (2-2)	L	1-3	89-56	2	-3.5	ATL
-	9/16	OFF DAY						2	-4.0	ATL
146	9/17	N	at CIN	SWIFT (18-8)/Roper	W	13-0	90-56	2	-4.0	ATL

147	9/18	D	at CIN	Burkett (19-7)/Pugh	W	6-1	91-56	2	-3.0	ATL
148	9/19	D	at CIN	Sanderson (4-2)/Ayala	W	7-3	92-56	2	-3.0	ATL
149	9/20	N	at HOU	Deshaies (2-2)/Swindell	W	7-2	93-56	2	-2.5	ATL
150	9/21	N	at HOU	PORTUGAL/Torres (2-3)	L	0-6	93-57	2	-3.5	ATL
151	9/22	N	at HOU	Swift (19-8)/Harnisch	W	1-0	94-57	2	-2.5	ATL
152	9/23	N	at HOU	Burkett (20-7)/Drabek	W	7-0	95-57	2	-2.5	ATL
153	9/24	N	S.D.	Beck (3-1)/Ge. Harris	W	4-3 (10)	96-57	2	-1.5	ATL
154	9/25	D	S.D.	Torres (3-3)/Ashby	W	3-1	97-57	2	-1.5	ATL
155	9/26	D	S.D.	Swift (20-8)/Brocail	W	5-2	98-57	2	-1.5	ATL
156	9/27	N	S.D.	Burkett (21-7)/Benes	W	8-4	99-57	2	-1.0	ATL
157	9/28	N	COL	Hickerson (7-5)/Nied	W	6-4	100-57	T1	-	ATL
158	9/29	D	COL	Reed/Torres (3-4)	L	3-5	100-58	2	-1.0	ATL
159	9/30	N	at L.A.	Swift (21-8)/Candiotti	W	3-1	101-58	T1	-	ATL
160	10/1	N	at L.A.	Burkett (22-7)/R. Martinez	W	8-7	102-58	T1	-	ATL
161	10/2	D	at L.A.	Brantley (5-6)/Hershiser	W	5-3	103-58	T1	-	ATL
162	10/3	D	at L.A.	KE. GROSS/Torres (3-5)	L	1-12	103-59	2	-1.0	ATL

POST ALL-STAR GAME RECORD: 44-29

FINAL 1993 RECORD: 103-59

Pitcher's name in ALL CAPS indicates complete game performance.

( ) - Indicates extra-inning game.